COLLECTING YOUR FEE

Getting Paid
from **Intake** to **Invoice**

E D W A R D   P O L L

Defending Liberty
Pursuing Justice

LawPracticeManagementSection

MARKETING • MANAGEMENT • TECHNOLOGY • FINANCE

Commitment to Quality: The Law Practice Management Section is committed to quality in our publications. Our authors are experienced practitioners in their fields. Prior to publication, the contents of all our books are rigorously reviewed by experts to ensure the highest quality product and presentation. Because we are committed to serving our readers' needs, we welcome your feedback on how we can improve future editions of this book. We invite you to fill out and return the comment card at the back of this book.

Cover design by Jim Colao.

Library of Congress Cataloging-in-Publication Data
Poll, Edward.
   Collecting your fee : getting paid from intake to invoice / Edward Poll.
     p. cm.
   ISBN 1-59031-153-1
   1. Lawyers—Fees—United States. 2. Collecting of accounts—United States. I. Title.
KF316 .P65 2002
346.7307'7–dc21

                                          2002153406

10 09 08 07 06   5 4 3 2

Discounts are available for books ordered in bulk. Special consideration is given to state bars, CLE programs, and other bar-related organizations. Inquire at Book Publishing, American Bar Association, 321 N. Clark Street, Chicago, Illinois 60610.

Contents

CHAPTER 6
Pricing as a Two-Way Contract with the Client   33

CHAPTER 7
Billing   39

CHAPTER 8
Technology   47

Foreword

When Ed Poll asked me to write the foreword to his new book, I thought the task would be easy. After all, a book's foreword is where you say a few nice things about the book, extol its author, and encourage the audience to read on. This would be easy, I thought. After all, having served as a general counsel for over a decade, I learned a little bit about paying legal bills. I went through over a hundred million's worth. And, having worked with Ed, I knew firsthand of his vast knowledge of the niche about which he had chosen to write, and the fact that so little has been written on the subject. I was only half right.

In this book, Ed demonstrates once again that the business of law is about a lot more than doing any one thing right. Getting clients to pay, like everything else in a well-run practice, is about running your practice right. It starts with choosing the right clients, setting the right expectations, and continues on through the entire representation. Ed's working premise is a favorite of the legal sector's best consultants: Getting paid is as much about achieving the highest levels of client satisfaction as it is about running your back room well. Being the lawyer that he is, Ed supports his premise with salient and practical advice about how to gear your practice so that clients happily pay their bills. But, being the consultant he is, Ed doesn't stop there. In the appendix, Ed gives you the well-tooled forms you'll need to implement his advice. This book is as much a field guide as it is a tactical strategic manifest for getting paid.

For everybody in professional services, in the end, getting paid is what it is all about. Not only does it put bread on the table, but we also all feel a certain "high" when a client pays the bill in full, quickly, with a note expressing thanks for outstanding service and results. At times like those, practitioners often reflect on what went right. Those who excel find ways to inculcate their reflections into every aspect of their practice. They discipline themselves and train their staffs on how to duplicate and improve upon their best practices. There are few resources for doing this. Many practitioners have created their own manuals, policies, and forms. If you've done this yourself, use this book as a benchmark to measure how well you've done. If not, save yourself the time. This book is a gift for you and those with whom you practice: your professional colleagues and those who assist you in your practice. It will save you countless hours, accelerate your learning curve, and reward you with the "high" of getting paid quickly by happily satisfied clients over and over again.

If you enjoy getting paid, and who doesn't, read on.

Peter Zeughauser
Zeughauser Group
Newport Beach, California

Preface

In a poll conducted by the National Federation of Independent Business (NFIB) and Wells Fargo, almost half of all respondents name their most significant problem as receiving late payments. When you add to that the phenomena of bounced checks, failure to receive full payment, and bankruptcy of customers, the domino effect can occur: Failure of customers' payments can cause bankruptcy of the vendor. Lawyers may face a similar situation.

Small business owners fall into the same trap as many lawyers. They tolerate late payments for fear of losing the customer or, in the case of the lawyer, the client.

When I was asked to write this book, I wondered what more I could contribute to this subject that I hadn't already discussed in articles and in my earlier work, *The Attorney and Law Firm Guide to The Business of Law,* Second Edition (ABA, 2002), in the chapters on pricing, billing, and collecting for your services. However, the more I spoke with colleagues and the more I thought about the subject, I realized that this area is a special niche that most people ignore. Most lawyers seek to get the clients and then do the work. We forget that the cycle isn't closed, the agreement between client and lawyer isn't completed, until we get paid. In fact, in many law firms, collection is almost an afterthought with as much as 30 to 40 percent of their billings collected in the *last two months* of their fiscal year.

Some people discuss this topic in terms of realization rate—a fancy way of saying that we received X percentage of that which we billed our clients. Thus, if we receive $68 for each $100 we bill, then we say our realization rate is 68 percent. Of course, if our realization rate—our rate of collection—is not 100 percent, we should wonder why. We should investigate the reasons why we are not able to collect for everything we bill. Is the reason our inefficiency, our ineffectiveness, our inertia? Or is the reason for failing to collect 100 percent a result of our client's unanticipated economic hardship, our client's unarticulated anger at the way we performed our services, or the malevolence of our client, which we failed to understand in our intake process?

We can control this area of endeavor to a greater degree than we think we can. The expectation and goal of this book is to provide some tools that will make your task a bit easier than in the past.

When we agree to perform services for our client, we (the lawyer *and* the client) are entering into a two-way bargain. We agree to perform legal services that meet or exceed the standard of the community and the expectations of the client, and the client agrees to pay us for our billings in accord with the terms of our written fee agreement. Anything short of this is a failure: generally (though not always) on our part!

Before going on, I want to thank Linda Ravdin for approaching me about writing this book; it has been more enlightening than I first imagined it would be. I want to thank Beverly Loder for her patience and understanding in helping me complete this work. It has been fun being reunited with her; she was my first editor on the very first work I completed for the ABA. My friend and colleague Wes Hackett has opened my eyes on a number of occasions and provided one of the best client-relations tools I have seen—the client status report—which appears in Appendix C. I want to thank him again for allowing me to show lawyers all over the country how easy it is to stay in contact with one's clients. And last, though certainly not least, I want to thank Heather Hutchins, my hands-on editor, without whom this work would not have been completed. I welcome your further thoughts and comments.

Edward Poll, J.D., M.B.A., CMC
http://www.lawbiz.com
(800) 837–5880
Venice, California

About the Author

Edward Poll, J.D., M.B.A., CMC, is a law firm management consultant, coach, educator, and speaker, helping lawyers all over the United States become more effective with their clients, more efficient, and more profitable.

Mr. Poll practiced law for twenty-five years and was CEO and COO of several manufacturing businesses. He has taught "Creating New Business Enterprises" in the Department of Entrepreneurship, University of California, Los Angeles (UCLA); created the "Business of Law Practice" for the University of Southern California (USC) Law Center for Advanced Professional Education; and was an instructor for the prestigious Institute of Continuing Legal Education (ICLE), formerly at the University of Michigan, Ann Arbor.

Mr. Poll is the author of several books, including *Attorney and Law Firm Guide to the Business of Law,* Second Edition (ABA, 2002); *Secrets for Buying and Selling a Law Practice,* Second Edition (Law Biz, 2002); *Secrets of the Business of Law: Successful Practices for Increasing Your Profits!* (Law Biz, 1998); *The Profitable Law Office Handbook: Attorney's Guide to Successful Business Planning* (Law Biz, 1996); and *The Tool Kit for Buying or Selling a Law Practice* (Law Biz, 1999). He is also the creator of the monthly audio subscription series, *Law Practice Management Review: The Audio Magazine for Busy Attorneys* (Law Biz, 2002).

Mr. Poll is a frequent contributor to legal and business publications, including *The Compleat Lawyer/GP Solo, Law Practice Management, Lawyers' Weekly USA, California Lawyer, Florida Lawyer, The Practical Lawyer, Law Office Economics & Management,* and *California Law Business* (supplement to the *Los Angeles Daily Journal*), among others. He also has been the moderator of various electronic seminars and online forums.

Ed Poll has the unique blend of twenty-five years of law practice (including civil litigation and corporate/business law) and more than ten years of helping lawyers become better at the business of law. Visit http://www.lawbiz.com and subscribe to the complimentary e-zine for additional information and ideas to become more effective, efficient, and profitable.

Introduction

1

It has been said that the love of money is the root of all evil. The want of money is so quite as truly.

—Samuel Butler

Lack of money is the root of all evil.

—George Bernard Shaw

Check enclosed.

—Dorothy Parker describing two of the most beautiful words in the English language.

In today's society, extension of credit is an art.

—Arthur Winston

CHAPTER CHECKLIST
- Improving the Relationship
- Preventive Medicine
- The History of Credit
- Different Perspectives on Debt
- You Are Not a Victim

§ 1.01 Improving the Relationship

When people in business, particularly those in the legal business, think of accounts receivable, they often think only of collection. Collecting accounts receivable is a process, and it begins the very first moment that you meet the client. It is built into the attorney-client relationship.

In fact, you can judge the success of your relationship with clients by the state of the client's account receivable. If the client pays each bill every month like clockwork, your relationship is working. However, if the client owes you a great deal of money and shows very little inclination to pay it, your relationship is clearly on the rocks.

Like a marriage, your relationship with the client must be built on shared expectations and two-way communication. This book is about improving your relationship with each of your clients and setting the proper expectations with new clients. Open communication, clear-cut expectations, goodwill on both sides, and follow-through will both improve your relationships with your clients and positively affect your bottom line—not to mention your cash flow. It has been said that you can judge the quality of a relationship by the way it ends. Payment on time of an account receivable by your client says that the attorney-client relationship has been good. The lawyer did the work; the client paid the bill. Both sides of the agreement were performed by the respective parties.

§ 1.02 Preventive Medicine

It may be helpful to think of this book in the same way that some people think of their daily dose of Echinacea and vitamin C: preventive medicine. Such a regimen tends to ward off disease. In a similar fashion, following the accounts receivable advice in this book will tend to ward off those 120-plus–day past-due accounts.

First and foremost, this is a book about creating good client relationships and thereby collecting a higher percentage of your billings. Some lawyers may find these two concepts anathemic to one another. But creating a good relationship with your client is a large part of collecting your accounts receivable. In fact, I would hazard you do not truly have a good relationship with your client unless the client's account receivable is up to date. If you do not have that kind of relationship with your client, the client does not really respect you. The client may be using you or hoodwinking you or playing you against a competitor, but a client who genuinely respects you and the work you do will pay your bill in a timely manner. We presume that the client can afford your service (that is, has not suffered economic reverses) and is satisfied with your service and its result. Read more on client attitude matching timely payment in Chapter 2.

Most, if not all, insurance carriers advise their insureds not to sue clients for past-due, unpaid fees. This book is not a primer on suing your clients for the money they owe you. Litigation for unpaid fees is a last-ditch approach. When all else fails, I favor this approach—but only after complete review of your file and serious consideration of all factors. We will discuss this last resort later.

§ 1.03 The History of Credit

The basic definition of credit is the power or ability to obtain goods or services now in exchange for a promise to pay for them later. The notion of future payment is embedded in the process as is the concept of risk. In every transaction of credit, the lender assumes some risk dependent upon the probability that the promise of payment will be fulfilled.

This idea of credit is a relatively new invention. As late as the year 1300 it was illegal to charge interest on a debt. That changed with the Renaissance. The Medicis and the Rothschilds were moneylenders of great wealth. At that time, credit was used only in mercantile transactions from one business to another. The modern concept of consumer credit arose in the nineteenth century.

In the middle of the nineteenth century, businesses learned to market themselves to consumers, and the idea of granting credit to customers so that they could buy your products began to take shape. Today, there are companies who do nothing but grant credit to consumers, and they extract a hefty interest for doing so.

Credit, however, is different from debt. Credit is a power, capacity, or ability. Wealth, for example, is any material or physical object that satisfies human wants provided that the object is limited in amount. Gold, diamonds, and platinum fall into this category. Credit is a special means whereby a person can acquire the right to use wealth that he or she does not have.

§ 1.04 Different Perspectives on Debt

There is an interesting dichotomy between the perceptions of bad debts in large versus small law firms. In large firms, the overall cost of an individual bad debt to each partner is small. This absence of pain is frequently reflected in the partner's attitudes toward collecting the debt and working for the client with the bad debt. In many instances, the partner in a large firm is less concerned with the status of the Account Receivable. In some larger firms, a penalty system has been installed to encourage the lawyer to pay more attention to the collection effort. Such carrot-and-stick systems have only inconsistent positive results for the firm.

On the other hand, lawyers in small firms or in solo practice feel the pinch of bad debts much sooner. Bad debt immediately affects the small firm's or solo practitioner's bottom line, which usually means immediate reduction of take-home pay.

How the small firm or solo lawyer reacts to the client responsible for the bad debt is conditioned upon his or her business experience. As in large firms, solo and small-firm practitioners will continue to work for the client in the misguided hope of being paid in the future. Others may continue to work for the client in order to preserve the relationship. Still others continue to work for the client in hopes of future work or of getting referrals from the client.

While lawyers must consider the entire client relationship, they should on no account be lulled into a false sense of obligation to clients who do not pay their bills. Clients respect firmness and a business approach, and clients generally do not make future referrals to lawyers they do not respect. As stated earlier, if the client respects you and the work you do, he or she will pay your bill in a timely fashion. The client will make payment of your bill a high priority.

Collecting accounts receivable starts at your very first meeting with the client and continues through the initial engagement, your work for the client, billing, and the final payment of the final bill. Your job is to set the expectation of payment from the very beginning. Explain your credit policy (you will create one in Chapter 2) and when you expect to be paid. Make it clear that you will stop work if you are not paid on time. And get the client to verbally agree and then to sign a written agreement about payment.

§ 1.05 You Are Not a Victim

Law firms are not the victims of their delinquent clients. You and the firm itself cause your collection problems by not telling clients from the beginning what you expect from them. Thus, you and your firm are the only ones who can solve your collection problems.

Firms fall into collection problems for a variety of reasons. Often an overriding fear is the loss of business. For this reason, partners accept work for clients who are unsuitable. Another reason for collection problems is that the firm has no written collections policy so each partner handles the collections differently. Firms can cause themselves collection problems because they refuse to use outside collection agencies to help them collect on their overdue accounts. All of these factors can lead to collections disasters.

Think of it this way: If you do not create a collections policy, your customers will do it for you. In fact, if you have trouble collecting your billings, they already have—and their version of your collections policy will not contribute significantly to your bottom line or cash flow.

You need to create a collections policy and stick to it. Only you and the lawyers in your firm can stem the flow of bad debts and overdue accounts.

§ 1.06 Action Plan

Get ready to collect a higher percentage of your billings.

Intake Process   2

*We all know how the size of sums of money appears
to vary in a remarkable way according as they are
being paid in or paid out.*

—Julian Huxley

Proper credit-checking will prevent a bad debt.

—Arthur Winston

CHAPTER CHECKLIST
- From the Beginning
- The Intake Interview
- Extending Credit
- Creating a Credit Application
- The Lawyer as Sleuth
- Creating a Credit Policy

§ 2.01 From the Beginning

The beginning of your relationship with the client is
by far the most important period. At your first meeting, you need to impress upon the client that you
expect to be paid. Lawyers are normally very good
about getting all the information needed to determine

if a conflict of interest exists. They are also quite competent at finding out enough information to decide if they have the right expertise to handle the case. The new skill of setting the right tone to get paid is a knack that lawyers can easily learn if they want to.

First, lawyers have to make sure that the client is listening. Often clients come to lawyers because of a problem. The problem is so troublesome that the client cannot handle it personally and must contact a lawyer. The problem can so consume the client that the client cannot really hear what you are saying. To counteract this difficulty, lawyers need to adopt a stance called "active listening."

In active listening, the lawyer listens to what the client says and paraphrases it back to the client. Then the client can clarify if the lawyer hasn't gotten it just right. The process forces clients to listen carefully to what the lawyer is saying so they can clarify if necessary. The wonderful by-product of active listening is that clients feel their problems have been really understood because everything they say is repeated back for their approval.

What goes without saying, but perhaps is worth saying anyway, is that active listening precludes the lawyer "talking at" the client. Clients do not respond well to this strategy, and they quickly tune the lawyer out. Active listening also forces the lawyer to be more attuned to the wishes (if not needs) of the client.

While you are using active listening to talk with your client, you can ask the usual questions about conflicts and the nature of their matter, but you also need to talk about your fees, your credit policy, your credit application, and the expectation that the client will pay the bill upon receipt. You may want the client to repeat or paraphrase back to you as well, just to confirm the client was also listening. When each of you repeats back the other's comments about all of this, you will know that each party understood what the other was saying. Do not worry about not having a credit policy or credit application: You'll be creating them in this chapter.

§ 2.02 The Intake Interview

During your very first meeting with each client, discuss the issue of fees. Bring it up yourself. Clients will appreciate your candor and be delighted not to have to bring it up themselves. The issue of your fees will be something the client had already considered, and it is much better to discuss the issue immediately and up front than to allow it to become the elephant in the center of the room.

If you want to establish a good relationship with your client from day one, you need to anticipate your client's concerns. At the first meeting, your fees will be important to the client. Moreover, the first meeting is the best possible time to make your policies about fee payment clear to your client. True, you may not have payment policies in place yet, but you will by the time you finish this book. Conduct that initial interview with your client as if you will have a collection problem in the future.

Yes, you read that correctly. Act as if the client will develop into a slow payer or a nonpayer or a payer who promises great things and delivers only minor ones. Do this for one reason and one reason alone: because the exercise will make you extremely clear about what you expect from the client. In Chapter 3, we will talk about fee agreements that you and the client will sign, but for now be clear what you expect from the client and what the client can expect from you. Tell the client now that if you are not paid in a timely fashion, you reserve the right to stop working for the client—in fact, you will stop working.

This is also a good time to ask about the client's expectations. You may greatly surprise the client by asking.

§ 2.03 Extending Credit

The best collections policy is to collect cash up front, or payment in advance of doing the work. This is a great theory but seldom can be accomplished. Clients may be accustomed to making a deposit against future services, yet the lawyer's billing in the first month will normally exceed the retainer, no matter how large the retainer was.

The patient may be accustomed to paying the doctor and dentist at the time services are rendered; the client is not so accustomed to paying the lawyer in the same manner. However, when the lawyer is able to ask for and receive an advance before beginning work, no matter how small the retainer, the lawyer will have eliminated many potential deadbeats.

A large retainer is seldom possible. Our commercial society is just not built this way. Insistence on full payment or large retainers in advance of performing our services would result in substantially less work. Most clients do pay their bills in full, especially when we employ the collection techniques suggested in this book, and feel insulted when they are not trusted to fulfill their payment obligations.

As lawyers, we extend credit to our clients. Most of us accept the client and do work on that client's behalf without any real certainty that the client will pay us. Without appropriate collections policies and procedures in place, we should not be surprised if we find out later that the client pays slowly or does not pay at all.

In order to get paid on a regular basis, lawyers need to take a more businesslike approach to extending credit. One survey concluded that it takes an average of 121.9 days for a law firm to collect on a bill. Fortune 500 companies do it in an average of 39.6 days. One way to collect in a timely fashion is to make the process of extending credit conscious to both the client and lawyer, to make it public. Such a public and obvious extension of credit involves a credit application that the client has to fill out.

If the client balks, that's a first-rate clue as to the client's intention of paying you. Clients have to fill out credit applications to get supplies from vendors and to get credit from the bank and even health-care providers. Why shouldn't they fill out such applications for you? You can always tell them that you are perfectly happy to accept cash—up front, of course. Short of that, because you are extending credit just like doctors and other professionals, the credit information they provide to other professionals must also be given to you.

In reality, good customers will see your credit policy and the credit application in a positive light. For one thing, you have brought the process out into the light where it becomes obvious that you know and the client knows that your law firm is extending credit from the first minute you begin work on a case. Your clients will value creating a relationship with a firm that is committed to sound business practices.

§ 2.04 Creating a Credit Application

A credit application does not need to have many more questions than the average New Client Intake Form. You want to know three types of information: general, financial, and reference. Several sample forms are provided in the appendices to this book. For this discussion, we have used the first sample intake form from Appendix A as Figure 1.

To start with, you will need the exact legal name of the client company, the street address (post office boxes will not work for a credit check) and the city, state, and ZIP code. Then you add the full legal names and titles of those who own the company if it is a proprietorship or partnership. If the company is a corporation, you want the name and title of an authorized officer of the company. You also need the home addresses and telephone numbers of these people. And be sure to get social security numbers: This can be especially helpful in locating and identifying people later. The last piece of general information you need is contact names. What is the name, title, telephone number, and email address of your day-to-day contact for payment of bills? At this time, get the name of a higher-up in the company: someone who has authorization to cut a check, for example. You want to know this person by name in case things go really wrong.

Financial information you will need includes trade references and banking information. As with all references that people supply willingly, expect to get the names and addresses of the company's best friends, the solo proprietor's brother-in-law, or the partner's golf buddy. Banking information is easier, but you want to know the name and telephone number of the bank officer who is in charge of the account. Ask if the client would prefer to pay by credit card and, if so, obtain the appropriate information with specific authorization to charge the credit card each month.

You want to ask a few other questions that are not strictly financial. For example, you want to know:

◆ how old the company is;
◆ in what state is it incorporated;
◆ the names of the officers of the company;

Figure 1
New Client Intake Form 1

Date _____

Full Legal Name of Firm: _____

Street Address: _____

City: _____ State: _____ ZIP Code: _____

Full Name and Address of Owner(s) or authorized corporate official

_____

_____

Federal Tax ID # or SSN: _____

Driver's License Number: _____

Reason for Leaving Last Law Firm:

_____

_____

Type of Company:

❒ Proprietorship ❒ Partnership ❒ Corporation

Age of Company: _____ State of Incorporation: _____

Contacts:

Name of Contact for Credit and Collections:

_____

Telephone Number: _____ Email: _____

Name of Contact for Check Authorization:

_____

Telephone Number: _____ Email: _____

Trade References:

Name	Title	Telephone

Name	Title	Telephone

Name	Title	Telephone

Bank References:

Name	Street	State and ZIP Code

Name of Bank Official Responsible for Account:

_____ Telephone Number: _____

Applicant's signature attests financial responsibility, ability, and willingness to pay our invoices in accordance with the following terms.

Firm Name _____

By _____ Title _____

By _____ Title _____

- names of the owners;
- why the client left the last law firm (the answer you receive may not be the truth, but it will certainly give you some insight into the company); and
- how much work this client will have for your firm (it is quite possible that the client will not have any idea).

Somewhere at the bottom of your credit application, you should have a sentence to this effect: *Applicant's signature attests financial responsibility, ability, and willingness to pay our invoices in accordance with the following terms . . .* Then you explain your terms: net 30 days or net 45 days or payable upon receipt. This sentence about financial responsibility may be unique to your firm or practice, but like the credit application itself, it makes the issue of credit explicit in your relationship.

While I advise against charging interest, if you are planning to charge interest on any unpaid balances, this form is the place to mention it. The ability to do this will vary from state to state. And if your state allows you to charge interest, please make sure to put the information somewhere in the middle of the form and make it bold. You do not want clients to miss this vital piece of information. In fact, you will want to go over the form with clients as they fill it out. Remember, two-way communication will make your entire relationship—and especially the collections process—go well. You may even request that clients initial individual sentences or paragraphs that are particularly important.

§ 2.05 The Lawyer as Sleuth

Another suggestion to find out how well the company is doing is to train yourself to be as clever as any of the mystery sleuths you read about. John Grisham and Scott Turow and others have written wonderful thrillers about the legal profession, so why can't you and your colleagues become sleuths in a business fashion?

The best possible way to understand the client's business is to visit him or her at the place of business. Not only does this ingratiate you to the client, but also it gives you an amazing opportunity to snoop. While you are getting your personal tour of the plant, scan the inventory and pick up the names of other suppliers. The client will give you as references the names of the vendors they always pay on time. You want to know how the other vendors are treated.

Look at the physical condition of the business. Is the building in good condition? Do the employees look busy? Does the work seem orderly? Are people standing around? Are employees wearing appropriate safety devices? These visual signals can give you clues about the viability of the business while also helping you advise the client on legal matters. Does the company, for example, want to hear about safety issues from your plant tour or from the OSHA supervisor who is following up on a complaint? You are snooping to find problems of a legal nature as well as problems with the client's credit.

Another good way to find out about a client's business is to simply ask questions. I haven't met a business owner yet who did not want to talk about his or her business—endlessly. So ask questions. No one expects you to understand the intricacies of every type of business even if you are a corporate lawyer. Clients love to be the experts, so ask them about the processes you are seeing. While the client is explaining the ins and outs of the metal-stamping business, he or she is also telling you exactly what you want to know about how the business is doing, who the competition is, and what the future looks like for the company.

§ 2.06 Creating a Credit Policy

After asking clients to fill out your firm's credit application, there are three basic parts to setting a credit policy:

- ◆ You approve clients for credit.
- ◆ You determine credit limits.
- ◆ You set interest rates.

Approve Clients
If you evaluate your client's worthiness for credit right at the beginning, you will save a great deal of time and money later on. You can check customers through LEXIS/NEXIS, Dun & Bradstreet,

the National Association of Credit Managers, industry trade reports, or credit-rating agencies such as TRW (http://www.truecredit.com), Equifax (equifax.com), Experian (experian.com), and others.

You can even ask clients to bring in their own credit report or charge a nonrefundable application fee, which you use to run a credit check. Because this will become the cost of doing business with every client, you may consider building the cost into your fee structure.

However you decide to handle the specifics in your firm, be sure to use at least two or more sources of information. One source is hardly doing proper due diligence on the creditworthiness of the client. Two or three different sources are more likely to give you a complete picture of the client's business. And recheck the client's credit every year. In fact, try to visit the client's business at least once a year at the same time that you rerun the credit check. Your visual appraisal of the business may tell you more than the credit check.

Determine Lines of Credit

Set credit limits for each client and stick to them. In larger firms, the lawyers who are rainmakers often work special favors for their best clients and cause the firm to bend the rules. If you genuinely want clients to pay their bills on time, make few or no exceptions. The decision that you make in the middle of some fevered frenzy of work for the client may make it impossible for you to walk away from that client later on. Either you will not want to walk away or the court may not allow you to do so because the trial date is imminent. As I like to continually remind myself, involuntary servitude begins with the failure to set appropriate credit limits.

Set Interest Rates

It seems counterintuitive to set interest rates for clients who are slow to pay. After all, if the clients could pay, they would pay their bill on time. Moreover, if you cannot convince clients to pay on time, you will certainly find it impossible to convince them to pay the interest on the bill they could not pay. It is for these reasons that charging interest may be more of a bookkeeping headache than it is worth. But charging an interest rate may be a deterrent to nonpayment. If you intend to charge interest, include that information on your credit application and, later, in your fee agreement to bring the issue of credit and the granting thereof to the forefront. Check the rules in your jurisdiction as to the amount of interest you may charge clients. Rates are often different for individual and corporate clients.

Clearly, the best possible scenario is for the client to pay each bill as soon as it becomes due. Resist the urge to extend credit as a sales tool. Credit that you extend when business is slow is credit you will regret later.

§ 2.07 Action Plan

- ◆ Create your credit application.
- ◆ Create your credit policy.
- ◆ Put your credit policy in writing and make sure that every lawyer in your firm abides by its rules.

Acceptance of Representation

3

CHAPTER CHECKLIST

- ◆ Fee Agreement
- ◆ Engagement Letter
- ◆ Withdrawing

§ 3.01 Fee Agreement

To fully address the client's part of this agreement, the lawyer should prepare a letter separate from the engagement letter and have the client sign and date it. This separate letter should detail the firm's hourly rates and the client's agreement to pay the firm's bills upon receipt. See the example letter in Appendix C at the end of this book.

Attach to this letter the names and billing rates of those likely to work on the client's matter. Include associates and paralegal staff as well as senior partners who may be expected to work on the matter as billable professionals.

In this letter, describe the firm's billing process, the fees, the collection process, and any interest that you will charge on unpaid balances. Explain that you expect clients to pay the firm's bills upon receipt. If you have a policy of reviewing and revising fees periodically, such as annually, say so at this point. Further, provide that no new fee will be implemented without advance notice to the client. (Special note: Be careful not to be seen as taking advantage of a client who may feel that he can go nowhere else after you have begun to handle his matter and now are increasing the billing rate. You may want to find a way to gradually ease into the new rate with existing clients, or get their affirmative consent before implementing the new rate.)

Insert a signature box or line beside every significant paragraph for the client to initial that he or she has read, understands, and will abide by the firm's policies. Ask the client to sign the letter at the bottom, too, with an appropriate line saying that *by signing this letter the client understands the firm's fee structure and agrees to abide by the firm's billing policies as set forth in this letter.*

This fee agreement is another means of making it clear to clients what you expect from them. As with the credit application, it lets clients know that you follow sound business practices. It's also an insurance policy for the future. Should you ever have to take your client to court to get your fees, this letter will verify that the client agreed to abide by your firm's billing and fee policies.

The fee agreement is also the appropriate place to state in writing that you will withdraw from the client's matter if you are not paid in a timely fashion. Spell that out clearly here and ask the client to initial it. Discuss it with the client. Few people stay in business long if they continue to provide services to those who do not pay them. Most people understand this intuitively. Your job is to take this fact from the invisible realm of the intuitive and make it manifest. You are merely establishing the client's expectations of your behavior.

State requirements vary; check your local jurisdiction for what other issues may be required in your fee agreement. You may wish to include sections on arbitration or mediation between the client and your firm should a disagreement arise. Include a section to cover any incentives your firm will accrue if you win your case. In that instance, clearly define what "winning" would mean in the client's particular matter. Is it forcing the other side to settle for a smaller amount or actually winning the verdict in court? Be sure that your definition of winning and the client's definition are the same.

In the fee agreement, explain how the firm advances costs for the benefit of the client. List those fees and their usual amounts. Which of these costs would the firm expect to be reimbursed in the event of no clear victory in the case? Make sure that the client understands the nature and anticipated amount or range of these expenses and initials these paragraphs. This is also a good place to explain the firm's policy on air travel. Do your lawyers fly first class or coach when traveling on client business? Take the time to define in writing what your firm does and why. If you are concerned about being paid for these costs later, ask the client to initial the paragraphs.

§ 3.02 Engagement Letter

Most firms have a policy about written engagement letters, but the policy is often honored in its breach. "The failure to spell out the scope of the engagement in writing is probably the single most important omission made by lawyers," says Harold Stotland, a creditors' rights partner with Teller Levit & Silvertrust, P.C., of Chicago. Think of it this way: Because the most important part of your relationship is the legal work that you will do for the client, shouldn't you protect this part of your relationship as well?

Just as you want to make the issue of credit clear to the client, you want to clearly delineate what exactly you plan to do for the client and when you plan to do it. If you want to maintain the good relationship you already have with the client, you will want the client to know and agree to every step of your legal plan. You want the client to buy into your legal approach.

Start by defining the matter the client has brought to you. Explain the steps you plan to take to resolve the matter to the client's satisfaction. As with the fee agreement, ask the client to initial the most important paragraphs. Using active listening, make sure that the client understands each step of the process and the probable results. Be completely honest about what you expect to happen. If you allow the client to believe that you can win the case outright without settling and then you settle, the client may perceive that you did not do your job. A knowledgeable client is an asset to your work. Also, make it clear here at the beginning who decides when to settle the case or withdraw. You can advise the client for hours, but the final decision and the ramifications of that decision belong to the client. Make sure that the client knows this.

Another point to make in the engagement letter is how often you will communicate with the client or how the client should communicate with you. If you warn the client from the beginning that you will be busy every minute in court, the client will expect that it is a part of the process to talk with your support staff or assistant. If you empower your staff to give appropriate information to the client or update the client on a weekly or monthly basis, the client will not be calling you every few days to see how things are going. Let the client know what to expect and how to work with you.

Enumerate the firm's policy on keeping original client documents. I advise against keeping original documents. Keep copies of everything in the client's file, but send the original documents to the client for safekeeping. After all, the documents belong to the client. In addition, you may want to let the client know the firm's policy and schedule of file destruction, ensuring the client that nothing will be destroyed in advance of potential need. While you do not want to worry the client unnecessarily or provoke any suspicion of document mismanagement, it is helpful to let the client know that after a certain period of years the firm archives or destroys old files. If you explain the process to the client now and ask the client to initial the relevant paragraph, you will save yourself and your firm countless difficulties in the future. And, of course, you will let the client know that the file can be sent to the client's last-known address instead of being archived or destroyed. Remember, a knowledgeable client is an advantage throughout the representation process.

§ 3.03 Withdrawing

The engagement letter is also the perfect time to explain in writing what happens if you withdraw as the lawyer. Each jurisdiction is different, but you want the client to know what will happen to the matter if you withdraw. Again, think of this section as another insurance policy for the future. As you have made clear in your fee agreement, you can and will withdraw if the client does not pay the bill. This is another opportunity to make your position clear to the client.

Refer back to the fee agreement to discuss time and fees expended on behalf of the client at the moment of representation. Explain in the agreement what will be billed to the client including such things as photocopies and telephone calls. Explain how your fees are determined if you withdraw in advance of the desire of the client.

List who controls the case when the lawyer withdraws and what happens to the matter in court. Usually, the matter is back in the hands of the client, but be sure to explain the rules clearly. In addition, check the Rules of Professional Conduct in your local jurisdiction and explain to your client what the profession expects of you and what you expect of the client, including how and when you will be paid for work done to the date of withdrawal.

§ 3.04 Action Plan

- ◆ Create a fee agreement.
- ◆ Create an engagement letter.
- ◆ Write a firmwide policy that institutes the use of these forms for every client and every matter.

Informing the Client

4

Money is better than poverty, if only for financial reasons.

—Woody Allen

CHAPTER CHECKLIST
- ◆ Increasing Contact
- ◆ Informing the Client
- ◆ Obtaining Consent

§ 4.01 Increasing Contact

The fee agreement and the engagement letter were just the beginning. The best possible way to get paid when you send your bill is to get the client to buy in at every step of the process. If the client is asked to agree at every stage of the matter, especially in cases involving litigation, there is no cause for argument when the bill comes. The client has, in effect, told the lawyer to incur these expenses and spend the time pursuing this avenue or approach or group of tasks. And if the client should chance to forget his or her involvement in the decision, you will have signed documents to prove it.

§ 4.02 Informing the Client

Clients want to know what is happening with their matters. You can be reactive and wait for their inquisitive or angry telephone calls, or you can be proactive and tell them in advance how the case is going. Proactive lawyers send periodic status reports to their clients. If, like most lawyers, you use the former method, your clients will not be happy and will not be in any particular hurry to pay your bill when it comes due. The latter method makes clients happy. They feel that you care about them and their matters. They know exactly how things are going with the case, and they feel as if they have some say in the outcome. These happy clients are much more likely to pay your bill upon receipt.

I suggest that you send the initial status report no more than 30 days from the first meeting with the client. However, after that, it does not matter how often you send clients a status report on their case. You can send a report weekly, biweekly, or monthly as long as you tell clients from the very beginning how you will be reporting to them, receive their acceptance of the schedule, and consistently send the report as you have promised. You set the client's expectation and then you do as you say you will do. Creating happy, bill-paying clients is nothing more than good communication and consistent follow-through.

Status reports can be simple, one-page documents that identify the current status of the matter/case, results of events since the last report, expected events in the next 30 days, anything required from the client by the lawyer, and the financial status of the client's account. Status reports not only benefit the client by keeping the client informed, they also benefit the lawyer as a malpractice deterrent by forcing the lawyer to review clients' files regularly. For sample status reports, see Appendix D at the back of this book.

Besides giving clients status reports in a timely fashion, you need to send them copies of every document you receive and every document you send out. The client needs to feel as if he or she is in the loop of communication. Make it a policy that your staff sends copies of everything pertaining to the matter to the client. This serves as further proof—beyond your status reports—that you are working diligently for the client. Most clients are not lawyers themselves and do not understand the law business. What they do understand is that you are constantly communicating with them, which means that you are constantly working for them or thinking about their matter.

Another good way to inform the client is to keep a current accounts receivable report at your desk. Every time a client calls you and asks you to take on a new matter, you can check the report to make sure that the client's account is current. If the client is delinquent, this is the perfect opportunity for you to advise the client of the consequences of his or her failure to be current. You'll find out how to create such reports in Chapter 9.

§ 4.03 Obtaining Consent

In addition to communicating regularly, you need to obtain the client's consent for each and every step of the representation. You need to get that consent in writing, if at all possible. That means that you want the client to sign a letter agreeing that you should settle the matter or withdraw or continue your court appearances. With a signed letter, the client is less likely to say later that he misunderstood the legal ramifications of the decision to withdraw or that she never agreed to the settlement. For all intents and purposes, the client is your boss in this particular legal matter, and you need to get your boss's consent before you take action. Educated clients want a voice in the proceedings. When they get that voice, they are happy and generally pay their bills on time.

If you cannot get an agreement in writing from your client, get a verbal agreement. At your earliest convenience, draft a memo confirming your conversation and the action you took based on the client's approval. In the memo, alert the client that if you have misunderstood his or her wishes, the client must contact you within a certain, but reasonable, period of time. If you have not heard from the client by that time, you will understand that the memo is correct as you have sent it. This procedure makes it difficult for the client to say later that he did not tell you to take any action or that she disagreed with the course of action you suggested. At the very least, draft a memo to be put in the client's file explaining the action you took and the conversation you had with the client. This is a last-ditch effort at documentation. It is much better and wiser in the long run to get a written memo from the client or the client's signature on a memo you have written.

As I said before, it is important to treat every client as if he or she will be a problem in the future. If you assume this, you will have documentation to cover every single action you have taken during the course of your representation. Should the client sue you for malpractice, you will be able to show that the client was consulted at every step. Or, should the worst happen, and you sue the client for payment of your fees and the client counterclaims, alleging malpractice, you will be covered with adequate documentation.

§ 4.04 Action Plan

- ◆ Tell clients from the beginning how often you will give them status reports on their cases.
- ◆ Send clients copies of all documents pertaining to their matters.
- ◆ Get clients to agree to every action in writing.

Budgeting 5

Money is like a sixth sense without which you cannot make a complete use of the other five.

—W. Somerset Maugham

CHAPTER CHECKLIST
- Reasons for Budgets
- Creating a Budget
- Agreement from Clients
- Payment Concerns

§ 5.01 Reasons for Budgets

Lawyers do not like budgets. Creating them can be difficult, as it is hard to know exactly how much time any particular task will take in corporate matters. Litigation is another world entirely. Unfortunately, clients are used to budgets. Most of them must operate within one every year. They are used to deciding upon a course of action based on the budget for that particular project. Clients assume that legal matters will fit into the same neat little box as the yearly advertising allotment or the annual revenue projections. Those involved in construction do not understand how it is possible to build a complex high-rise structure, with many different trades, in accord with a budget but not be able to project and estimate legal costs for a single matter.

While lawyers would like to skip the issue of budgets altogether and tell clients that legal work costs what it costs, that answer is no longer practical or accepted by corporate America. Perhaps in the 1980s when there were plenty of clients for every law firm this was a reasonable policy. However, the 1990s were an era of change for law firms. Almost every firm reduced the number of lawyers, and firms were managing their practices with fewer legal resources. The new century marks a coming of age for our profession. We are finally meshing the professionalism of our work with the necessities of the business world on a conscious level.

Clients want budgets. If lawyers want to keep their old clients and add new ones, they will need to begin to think about budgets. Two types of budgets in particular need attention: the overall budget for a matter and a specific litigation budget for an ongoing client.

§ 5.02 Creating a Budget

Timing is critical when creating a budget. Within 90 days of the trial, you are likely to spend four times as much of the client's money as you have beforehand. And, as with all other steps in the representation process, you need to get buy-in from the client.

Once you and your firm have decided to accept the client's case and you have approved the client through your firm's credit check, you will need to review the notes from your initial interview with the client. From this information, you can determine what sort of documents you will need the client to provide for the case. At this time, you can also think about how the case is likely to proceed.

Know Your Case/Matter

The most important factor in creating a realistic budget is to know your case. If you know your case, then you know what is reasonable to expect in the course of the proceedings and what is reasonable to expect from the client. It is unlikely that this will be the first time you have handled a matter like this. You have worked on similar cases, and you know what is likely to occur.

Given your experience and the information you can gather, come up with a matter or case plan. This will then facilitate creating a budget of how much time you think the case will take. Be sure to include your time in court, time to strategize, and time to research. That is just *your* time. Now figure out how much time you will need from your assistant, your associates, and your paralegals. And do not forget experts, consultants, and out-of-pocket costs. If it helps you, consider two budget scenarios: the best-case scenario in which everything goes exactly as you wish and the worst-case scenario in which everything that can go wrong does.

Now do the math. How much will your time cost in the best scenario? How much in the worst scenario? Figure out the costs of your staff for both scenarios. Will you need to create presentations for court? Will you need to use technology in court? Will you need hundreds of copies? Add these costs in and any other items that you can think of that will apply. See the sample budgets in Appendix E.

Now comes the hard part. You have to explain your plan and budgets to the client.

Educate the Client

Tell the client exactly what you expect to happen and explain your two budget scenarios. Do not paint a rosy picture or shield the client. Some lawyers will not admit that they could lose the case or that elements outside their control (the judge, the jury, or the opposition) could unfavorably affect the outcome. Most clients are business-savvy enough to know that you cannot predict the future. They do not expect you to. All they want is some idea of the options, probable outcomes, and corresponding costs involved. They are used to making educated guesses about the future of their businesses, and they expect you to be able to make educated guesses about their matter and your business.

The issues of time and money will matter greatly to clients. That is why you have created two scenarios. Obviously, the actual cost of the matter will be somewhere in between the best scenario and the worst one. The important point is to walk your client through each scenario. By doing this, you are, in effect, telling the client what to expect each step of the way. Getting buy-in from the client helps both you and the client.

§ 5.03 Agreement from Clients

Now you need to get the client to agree to both your course of action and your budget. The simplest way to do this is to ask the client to sign at the bottom of your budgets and initial the key paragraphs. Getting the client involved is imperative. The reasons for this are fairly obvious, but they bear repeating.

Client's Right to Know

The client is not your friend nor yet an adversary, but the client has the right to know your honest thoughts about the case before you take any action. What the client is paying for is your expertise and legal opinion. That opinion is useless to the client unless you can articulate it so that the client understands what the legal action or lack of legal action will mean. You owe the client your honest appraisal of the legal problem and the probable outcome.

No one is asking you to predict the future, but your acute legal judgment and experience can offer the client some guidelines as to the result. The client will take whatever action he or she deems necessary. Your job is to advise the client to the best of your ability.

The Client Is an Integral Part of the Process

Although many lawyers wish it were otherwise, your client is part of the representation process. In fact, your client is the root of the representation process. Without the client, you would have no billings and thus no income. The client is not a necessary evil in the legal process. The client is the font of all you hope to achieve in your career. Without the client there are no court actions, no matters, and no victories . . . and no revenue!

The Buyer Has Final Approval

As noted earlier, the client is in a sense your boss during the representation process. Lawyers do not usually like to think of it that way, so it may be easier to consider the notion that the client, as the buyer, has the final approval of what is bought. In this case, the commodity is your legal services.

The more the client actually thinks of your legal service as a commodity, the more likely the client will delay payment. Because the client thinks of the service as a commodity, the client will perceive that anyone can do what you did and, as a result, there is no special hurry to pay the bill. Yet, where the client perceives that your service is special or is a bet-the-company type of service, you can be sure the client will be far more sensitive about assuring prompt payment of your bill. The client will want to make sure that you continue working on his or her behalf. This is one reason why law firms today are seeking to differentiate themselves in their marketing efforts from other law firms and lawyers.

However, in a more practical vein, you need the client's approval of everything you do for one reason: If you fail to get the client's approval in advance, there will almost always be a fee dispute or discount at the end of the representation process. If you want to be paid, especially if you want to be paid upon receipt of your bill, you need to get the client's approval in advance every step of the way.

§ 5.04 Payment Concerns

You have already asked the client to fill out a credit application and sign a fee agreement. You have assigned the client a credit limit. However, if you are still concerned about your client paying the bill, you need to do two things.

Determine Client's Ability to Pay

First, determine your client's ability to pay. How did the client react when you discussed the budget for the case? You are well within your rights to ask how the client plans to pay for the budget you have sketched out. However, most lawyers feel uncomfortable asking such questions. You can do another credit check. You can check with the client's bank. You can call the client's references or suppliers. If these inquiries do not answer your nagging questions, then you can ask for a retainer in advance of proceeding further.

Get Retainer in Advance

If you are genuinely concerned that your client may not have the money to pay you, ask for a retainer in advance. You can do this right after showing the client your budget. Because the budget will be a certain amount, you require a certain percentage of that in advance to work on the matter. At the time you request the retainer, you also need to be clear about maintaining a reserve. Many lawyers specify the minimum balance that the client is required to maintain in the retainer account. If the balance should drop below this minimum level, the lawyer will withhold services or withdraw from the case. Of course, be sure to consult your jurisdiction's Rules of Professional Conduct to be sure you do not prejudice the client's interest if you pause in your service or withdraw.

While you can cover all of this in your fee agreement, it may only be appropriate to mention it once you have worked out the plan and budget for the client's case. In some cases, you may produce the budget before agreeing to represent the client and therefore include the budget as a separate letter to be signed along with the fee agreement and engagement letters. Otherwise, you should discuss the budget as soon after your engagement as possible. This definitely should be within the first 90 days of your engagement before you are too committed.

§ 5.05 Action Plan

- ◆ Create a best-case and a worst-case budget for your client.
- ◆ Discuss the budgets and your expectations with the client.
- ◆ Get the client to sign off on your budget.

Pricing as a Two-Way Contract with the Client

6

The question of fees is important, far beyond the mere question of bread and butter involved. Properly attended to, fuller justice is done to both lawyer and client. An exorbitant fee should never be claimed. As a general rule never take your whole fee in advance, nor any more than a small retainer. When fully paid beforehand, you are more than a common mortal if you can feel the same interest in the case, as if something was still in prospect for you, as well as for your client. And when you lack interest in the case the job will very likely lack skill and diligence in the performance. Settle the amount of fee and take a note in advance. Then you will feel that you are working for something, and you are sure to do your work faithfully and well. Never sell a fee note—at least not before the consideration service is performed. It leads to negligence and dishonesty—negligence by losing interest in the case, and dishonesty in refusing to refund when you have allowed the consideration to fail.

—Abraham Lincoln

CHAPTER CHECKLIST
◆ Pricing Is a Two-Way Agreement
◆ Responsibilities of the Lawyer
◆ Responsibilities of the Client
◆ Consequences

§ 6.01 Pricing Is a Two-Way Agreement

As noted in Chapter 2, lawyers incur expenses for their clients from the first moment of representation. Unless you ask for and receive a retainer in advance, you are working for the client on spec—meaning on the speculation that your client will pay you when the work is done. For this reason, it is important that the client agree to pay you in a timely fashion according to the requirements laid out in your fee agreement.

The intention from the lawyer's point of view is to create a two-way agreement with clear responsibilities on both sides. Pricing and payment is one way to find out if the client has taken the agreement seriously.

§ 6.02 Responsibilities of the Lawyer

The responsibilities of the lawyer are almost always crystal-clear to the lawyer, and there are Rules of Professional Conduct to back them up. The lawyer is to perform legal services for the client in accordance with these Rules. In addition to these professional responsibilities is the responsibility to communicate clearly with the client.

For more information about pricing issues, see Appendix F for the ABA's Model Rule on fees and Appendix G for the California State Bar rules on fees. Also see *Attorney and Law Firm Guide to the Business of Law*, Second Edition, by Edward Poll (ABA, 2002), especially the chapters on pricing, billing, and collection. In addition, see *The Essential Formbook, Volume II: Human Resources/Fees Billing and Collection*, by Gary A. Munneke and Anthony E. Davis (ABA, 2002).

§ 6.03 Responsibilities of the Client

The responsibilities of the client are often not as clear to the client as to the lawyer. The client is responsible to pay for the legal services he or she has contracted per the fee agreement that has been signed. Moreover, the client is responsible to pay within a certain period of time.

In addition, the client is supposed to cooperate with the lawyer. This includes providing information and documents in advance of the case and throughout the matter. The client also needs to participate in the process as a full member of the legal team. In this capacity, the client needs to understand his or her desires and needs as the legal process progresses. As these needs and desires change, the client is responsible to communicate them to the lawyer. The lawyer can then adapt the legal work to coincide with the changes in the client's needs.

§ 6.04 Consequences

When lawyers fail to perform their duties appropriately, they can be the objects of state bar proceedings and malpractice suits. These professional actions against the lawyer will diminish the lawyer's client base, get the lawyer fired, and perhaps cause the lawyer to be disbarred. All of these results will sully the lawyer's reputation, thereby making it difficult for the lawyer to continue in practice. These consequences of the lawyer's failing to live up to the two-way contract with the client are devastating. If the lawyer does not live up to the agreed-upon responsibilities, he or she can be ruined financially and professionally. The same cannot be said of the client who refuses to honor the two-way agreement.

When the client fails to live up to the responsibilities of paying the bill and participating in the legal process, sometimes nothing happens. That is why lawyers themselves need to create real consequences for the client.

Account Aging Report

Lawyers need to have a copy of the most recent Accounts Receivable Aging Report (explained in Chapter 9) on their desks at all times. This report clearly shows which clients are up to date with their bills and which have fallen behind. When clients call to ask the lawyer to take on more work, the lawyer must look at the report and discuss the results with the client. If the client is past due on the account, the real consequence is that the lawyer will not take on any new matters until the bill for previous legal services is paid in full.

Firing the Client

Another real consequence that lawyers can put into place is to fire the client if the client's account is past due. The lawyer sends the client a letter that informs the client that if the bill is not paid by a specific date, the lawyer will no longer continue to work for the client under the terms of the fee agreement.

Collection Efforts

Yet another real consequence involves the efforts to collect accounts receivable as described in this book. Make sure that the lawyer says what the next action will be if the client does not comply by paying the bill. Then the lawyer or the firm must follow through with the action that was promised. Never make a statement or threat that is illegal or not intended; and always take action in accord with your statement, including the time frame indicated.

Filing Suit

The final real consequence for the client will be when all collection efforts have failed, and the lawyer has to file suit to recover the billings. As the lawyer has explained in person and in the fee agreement, this is the final consequence if the client should not live up to his or her side of the bargain.

If we as lawyers have real consequences to our reputations and our livelihoods when we do not abide by the two-way contract with the client, why should clients be able to walk away from the agreement with no consequence at all? Clearly, they should not. However, it is up to the lawyers to set these client consequences in place, to document them in a fee agreement, and then to explain them clearly to the client and ask the client to sign the agreement.

The theme here is to make the two-way contract and the responsibilities on both sides visible to the client. The lawyer is well aware of the consequences should he or she fail to perform adequately. You must be sure that the client is also aware of the real consequences of his or her failing to perform adequately, which includes paying the lawyer's bill in a timely fashion.

§ 6.05 Action Plan

- ◆ Include real consequences to the client in the event that the client defaults on the agreement.
- ◆ Discuss these consequences with the client in the very first interview.

Billing 7

What's a thousand dollars? Mere chicken feed. A poultry matter.

—Groucho Marx

A billion here and a billion there, and soon you're talking about real money.

—Everett McKinley Dirksen

CHAPTER CHECKLIST
- Keeping Records
- Keeping Time
- Periodic Billing
- Billing Details
- Impact on Collections
- Marketing Opportunities

§ 7.01 Keeping Records

The most important and obvious fact about billing is that you cannot get paid until you send a bill to the client. However, the process for getting bills out differs in each firm. In order to get your bills out to clients as soon as possible, it is important that the entire billing process in your firm be streamlined. Most experts suggest that you record billable time at least every day instead of every week or every month.

Perhaps you have had the experience of a friend asking you at the end of the week what you did on Tuesday night. You stop. You try to remember. You went to work, but what did you do after work? Did you go straight home? Did you go out with friends? Did you have a business commitment? Several days after the fact, it is difficult to remember what you did.

The same situation applies to your billing records. On Friday, it may be just as difficult to recall which clients you worked for on Tuesday. More than that, clients prefer bills that they can understand. If you have trouble recalling which clients you worked for, how can you possibly recall exactly what you did for each client?

Daily record keeping is the easiest and most streamlined method of maintaining your records. Research has shown that if work is not recorded as it is completed, a certain percentage of time never gets recorded. That time is lost money for the lawyer and for the firm. Losing just one hour a day could cost the firm thousands of dollars. If you take that one hour a day and multiply it by a billing rate of just $100 per hour, the sum comes out to $500 a week or $26,000 a year in billings lost.

§ 7.02 Keeping Time

Management Tool

Keeping your time carefully is important to the firm and to your clients. The firm will use your billing information as a management tool. Are you billing the amount that you should every day? Are your notations clear and will clients understand what you actually did for them?

The firm will pay attention to your time sheets in order to know which cases are being worked on and which are not. In addition, the firm needs to collect data to know how many hours, on average, it takes for a given task in various kinds of matters. Some firms use this information to come up with cost-accounting practices to be used in the future for discussing and setting alternative fees. As stated earlier, the firm also wants to know the contribution (and perhaps compensation) of each lawyer to the firm.

Justification of the Fee

In addition to supporting the amount of your fee, another purpose of keeping your time is as a justification for your fee. When clients look at your bill, will they feel good about what you did for them? Will they be pleased that you have been working on their matter? If you drafted an important pleading for the client or a necessary brief, the client will probably feel that your fee is justified.

However, it is up to you to explain what you have done in words that the client will understand. Just noting that you reviewed the file for half an hour is not much of a justification unless you explain that the opposing counsel called with a new wrinkle in the case. Your half hour of review in the file not only answered the opposing counsel but also caused her to relinquish an earlier position. Explain that to the client, and you have not only worked hard but also justified your fee.

One thing that annoys clients at every level is the sense that their lawyer is nickel-and-diming them for every second spent on the case. Bill for a substantive legal service, a quality legal service, but not just for the five minutes it took you to look up a relevant fact. Show those five minutes on your bill, but indicate "no charge" (N/C). Clients will appreciate your courtesy and consideration. In fact, you could institute a policy at your firm. Choose not to bill clients for costs below a certain threshold—say, $5 or $10. The small costs that the firm would absorb will be more than offset by the increased goodwill of your clients.

Clients don't mind paying for lawyering, but they resent paying for endless consultations among lawyers and countless file reviews. If you want to keep your clients happy, try to think like them when you review your bill. Thinking like a client can help you in preparing a bill that demonstrates positively your value to the client and in continuing to maintain good client relationships.

§ 7.03 Periodic Billing

Monthly Billing

Most law firms bill on a monthly cycle. This makes perfect sense in the majority of cases. However, the firm should organize its billing cycle such that the bills arrive on clients' desks on or about the first or second day of each month. Arriving early in the month will ensure that the lawyer's bills are among the first ones paid during the month.

I have heard a variety of anecdotes about sending bills in brightly colored envelopes and enclosing brightly colored, preaddressed, stamped return envelopes. Several of my colleagues have suggested neon-pink envelopes, which hurt the eyes and can never get lost on the client's desk. Other colleagues use envelopes of blue or green. They say that the advantage of these specially colored envelopes is that it is easier to figure out which envelopes contain billings from the lawyer and which contain the usual assortment of junk mail and other materials. Also, when payment is made and it arrives in your office, you will know which envelope to open first.

More Frequent Billing

In certain specific situations, it makes sense to bill more often than once a month. For instance, in a large matter or case, it makes more sense to bill every two weeks. First, frequent billing keeps the client informed of the current costs of the matter. Second, it encourages frequent, though smaller, checks or payments by the client. Third, the firm has more money in its coffers. And fourth, the firm will know well in advance if the client is going to pay or not. In addition, the bills are yet another chance to keep in contact with your clients. In this fashion, clients, too, can keep better track of the money being spent on their matter.

In addition to large cases, billing more frequently is also a good idea when the client's financial stability is in question. Billing every two weeks enables the firm to get the fees quickly. In addition, it is often easier to collect smaller amounts over time than a huge amount at the end of the case. Also, human nature is such that the client is much more likely to pay when the case is ongoing.

The client still needs you, in fact. This more-frequent billing also keeps the final bill smaller like a reserve in a construction contract. If there is a dispute at the end, you are fighting over a smaller amount.

A final situation that may bear more frequent billing is when the lawyer is a solo practitioner or a small firm that cannot finance the entire matter for the client even in the short term. In this case, frequent billing will ensure that the firm or solo lawyer is not spending a great deal out of pocket.

Positive-Result Billing

Another type of billing to consider is positive-result billing, that is, billing when you have achieved a positive result for the client. When something good has happened in the case or matter, the client is at the top of the client satisfaction curve and less likely to be offended by the amount of your bill. After all, your bill was for the services required to achieve the good result and ultimately achieve the client's goal.

§ 7.04 Billing Details

First and foremost, your bills should be dignified and appropriate to the tone of your office or practice. The actual style can be almost anything that you can imagine. However, it is also important to make sure that your bill looks like a bill and not a letter.

A dignified presentation is good but only if the invoice also includes the three basic components that your clients will need to actually pay the bill:

- ◆ the date,
- ◆ the word "invoice" or "statement" printed in large letters and centered in the middle of the page, and
- ◆ a due date.

A good due date is approximately ten days beyond the date shown on the invoice. These basic pieces of information make it possible for the client's accounting staff to set the invoice up for immediate payment. In fact, some firms have found that merely including this information prominently has improved their cash flow.

In addition to basic information, a bill should include clear and understandable descriptions of what the lawyer has done. In today's world, clients prefer to pay for value, not time. Thus, it is incumbent upon the lawyer to describe the value he or she adds to the client. Though there may be periodic setbacks on a case, or even mixed results, there is almost always a positive element in your effort.

Start your description with the positive outcomes of your effort for the client. Clients will be more likely to see the positive, value-added benefits you have provided and will therefore be more likely to pay your bill in full sooner. The lawyering charges or fees should be separate from the paralegal charges and costs such as telephone or copy charges. Check the sample bill in Appendix H to see what I have in mind.

Many corporate clients have established written billing guidelines that they expect their outside counsel to follow in the formatting of billings. Outside counsel may not have a choice: They will either follow the guidelines or not get paid. Most clients, however, are reasonably flexible and will accept the lawyer's format as long as their prescribed or required information is contained in the bill. In addition, some corporations prefer task-based billings. For more information on this topic, please refer to the *Uniform Task-Based Management System* created by the American Corporate Counsel Association and the American Bar Association Section of Litigation. The Uniform Task-Based Management System can be found online at http://www.abanet.org/litigation/litnews/practice/uniform.html.

With a large corporate client, it is a good idea to meet the person in charge of accounts payable. Take this person to lunch and ask a number of questions. Find out what information is needed to speed up accounts payable. What information should be on the bill? Where should the information be located on the bill? Find out if the bill has to be okayed by more than one person. If it does, make sure to send duplicate copies of the bill to everyone who will need to sign off on it. If your bill has to be forwarded from one person to another, valuable time will be wasted before you are paid. Find out everything you and your firm can do to make the job easier for the accounts-payable department. If you can make their job easier, your firm will be paid more quickly.

The bill should also be carefully checked for spelling and arithmetic errors. Nothing in the world makes clients angrier than having to call their lawyers to discuss the 122-hour day that a paralegal put in. Moreover, you don't want to do anything to keep that bill from getting into the payment clerk's hands. If someone has to call you because they don't recognize the wrong or misspelled lawyer's name or the amounts don't add up, that is another few days or a week or more that you don't get paid. Do not give your clients any reason whatsoever to delay paying you. You want to make the payment process as easy as possible for the client.

§ 7.05 Impact on Collections

A good, clear bill that the client can understand is much easier to collect than a garbled letter that gets sent out with cryptic notations as to what the lawyer has done all month. Think of it this way: Clients do not understand the legal business, and they find it difficult to tell if their lawyer is doing a good job or a bad one. However, as businesspeople, clients do understand what a bill is and what it should look like. In fact, most consumers of legal services (clients) probably think they know a good bill from a bad one. If possible or practical, ask your clients what information should be included and what format they would prefer on the bill. No matter what billing format is used, make sure that your bills are clear, easy to read, and simple to understand. These three details will go a long way in getting your clients to pay their bills.

§ 7.06 Marketing Opportunities

Most lawyers are missing the hidden opportunity that bills represent. In addition to the status reports and letters that you send to your clients every month, your bill is the single most obvious way that clients see what you are doing for them. Don't waste this valuable opportunity to look good to your client. Explain carefully what you did for the client on each day. Write in complete sentences. Make sure that you haven't fallen into some sort of legalese, which will seem like so much annoying jargon to your clients.

You have worked diligently for the client all month, so show him that. Remind her of all the telephone calls you have made to the other side's lawyers. Jog his memory about all those impressive-looking legal documents you have been sending week in and week out. And describe what you have achieved for the client in each event.

Clients don't always understand the legal letters or documents you send them, but your bill is a good way to explain what you have been doing for the client to deserve all that money. As I said earlier, think of the bill as a defense of your fee. A client who reads your bill does not mind the large amount due at the bottom if he or she sees that you have been working hard and achieving positive results, which are moving the client closer to his or her goal.

The bill is a wonderful marketing opportunity in that you can communicate to the client—in the client's language—what you have been doing for the client every day. If you do a good job in preparing the bill, the bill will remind the client that you were thinking about him and his matter or her case all thirty-odd days of the month. And, believe it or not, clients really appreciate that sort of effort.

§ 7.07 Action Plan

- ◆ Create clear, readable bills with detailed descriptions of the work you have done for the client.
- ◆ Think about billing clients two times a month instead of monthly.
- ◆ Consider sending your bills with preaddressed return envelopes in bright colors.

Technology 8

*Take care of the pence, and the pounds will take
care of themselves.*

—Proverb

CHAPTER CHECKLIST
- ◆ The Role of Technology in Accounts Receivable
- ◆ Factors to Consider Before Updating Technology
- ◆ What Accounts Receivable Technology Looks Like

§ 8.01 The Role of Technology in Accounts Receivable

I believe that accounts receivable is a function to be performed by human beings, not by machines. As I will explain at length in Chapter 9, collection letters do not work, and no amount of technology will result in collections. The only way to collect accounts receivable is with a person calling clients on the telephone. However, having said that, technology can help provide information that human beings will need to better manage the accounts receivable process.

One of the foremost benefits comes with the ability to prepare bills and send them to clients in a timely fashion. Many clients, especially business clients, close their accounts-payable function by the fifth of the month. Statements that are received in advance of the fifth get processed that month; others wait for payment processing until the following month. While no guarantee, getting billing statements into the hands of the client at an early date does tend to speed receipt of payment by the lawyer. Of course, the opposite corollary is also true: Failure to get the billing statement into the hands of the client at an early date tends to delay receipt of payment. Some lawyers even close their billing cycle between the twenty-fifth and twenty-eighth of the month in order to mail the billing statement on or before the first of the following month, thus ensuring receipt of the billing statement by the client before the fifth of the month.

Some firms send billing statements twice a month or even weekly in an effort to keep better control over their accounts receivable and also help even out their cash flow.

§ 8.02 Factors to Consider Before Updating Technology

Solo and small firm practitioners have a number of programs they can use to manage their accounts receivable process. Currently, these programs include TABS III, PCLaw, and others. It is crucial to choose billing or accounting software that is already complete in its release and has been widely adopted and successfully used.

No matter which program you choose for your firm or practice, there are many factors you will need to consider before you begin researching software. One such factor is how widely used is the new system and what kind of technical support will be available. You need to decide these issues inside your firm before you can figure out which software products will be able to meet your needs.

Needs Analysis

First, take a look at your time and billing process and do a needs analysis. Determine what steps or technology might be missing from your current methodology. What other steps or technology would your firm like to have? Think about the future needs of your firm.

How much growth does your firm expect? How will your current technology be able to deal with more lawyers or more clients? What will your firm's needs be several years from now with respect to time and billing?

Since time and billing software tends to outlast other software, any ill-timed or ill-managed changes can be traumatic to the entire firm. For this reason, you want to think carefully about what your firm will need in the upcoming years before you begin to research the available systems. Sometimes all the gee-whiz technology creates a need where none existed before.

Conversion

No matter how fast or efficient your new software is, it will not be able to accomplish anything until all your old data has been converted to the new system. Can the new system do this? If it can, will there be an extra charge for the service? Will the converted data need to be tweaked by the vendor or your staff? Data does not convert seamlessly no matter what the vendor promises.

This is an area that requires detailed due diligence before selecting any new system. Talk to actual users who went through a similar conversion process. Ask them to relate their experiences. What would they do differently if they had the chance to go back and try it all over again?

No matter how flawless those salespeople or end-users claim a billing software package to be, it is crucial to use your current billing system in tandem with your new software (or the new technology you have created) for several months. This double-entry precaution is necessary even if you are simply modifying your current software. Anything else is a recipe for disaster. If the system does not work as advertised, you could find yourself with two or three months' unbilled or incorrectly billed time, which will lead to both short-range and long-range collection problems. Phase out your old system and software on a planned, deliberate migration schedule.

Training

Before you select any system, ask about the training options. Your firm will need to train everyone who will use the new system. In addition, the lawyers within the firm should also get an overview of the software. They will, after all, be managing the results of the data input. Training is the one factor most often overlooked and is the most expensive element of any purchase.

Tech Support

Check out what support will be available once the software is installed. Ask specifically about days and times that tech support will be available and how much any such support will cost. Also ask about maintenance agreements to keep your software up and running. How much extra will this be?

Staffing

Will your new technology require the addition of new staff? Will you need to hire training personnel for a limited time? What will the cost factor be for any new staff?

Reporting

Before you even begin to look at software systems, determine what reports your firm wants to be able to produce. Do you want accounts receivable aging reports, date-of-last-payment reports, realization-rate reports, or time-code reports? Can the software produce these reports? Will you need a customized software program to get these reports? Be sure that your firm's basic needs are met before you find out what kind of extra reports the software can produce.

Hardware

Will you need new hardware to optimize the speed and effectiveness of the new software? Do you have it? Will you have to buy it? What will new hardware cost? How much training will be required to operate the new hardware and keep up its maintenance? Will the firm have to hire additional Information Technology staff?

Interfacing with Other Programs

After you have considered all of the other factors, you need to consider one last thing: How will any new time and billing programs work with other programs already in use in your firm? For example, will the new time and billing software interface with the marketing databases? After all, you will want to be able to send newsletters, invitations, brochures, and other marketing materials to your new clients as well as to your old ones. Will the two products be able to "speak" to one another or interface in the current computer jargon?

Before you spend hundreds or thousands of dollars or the same amount of hours, take a close look at all of the various in-house programs being used throughout your firm. Does the firm want to keep all of these different programs in use? Does the new software have the capability of "speaking" with these other programs? Whether or not the new software interfaces with the old software, the recommendation to continue to double-input with both new and old software bears repeating. Double-input of data may make running the firm harder for the adjustment period but will save countless billing crises in the end.

Buy-In

While technology is not the subject of this book, the issue of technology can often mask some more difficult problems within the structure of a law firm. In lieu of enacting real change and promoting honest communication in the way the firm approaches clients and billings, some firms will opt instead for buying newer or faster technologies that are expected to solve the problems of overdue bills altogether. If fundamental processes in time-keeping, billing, or collection are flawed, no software yet invented will fix them. As any software vendor will tell you, no matter how wonderful the software is, people still run it.

Before you or your firm buys any hardware, software, or any combination of the two, someone in your organization has to plan how to achieve buy-in from the firm. I write at length about getting buy-in from clients on fee agreements and letters of engagement. Buy-in from the lawyers and staff at your firm is just as vitally important. No matter how much money you spend on gee-whiz software, the bills will not go out even a minute quicker unless the people involved in the process actually use the software and use it correctly.

Buy-in is important for any change to "the way we've always done it" in a law firm. Even changes that do not require software or training will require willing participation by those involved. You cannot set up a new collection process, no matter how logical or obvious, without finding a way to get those involved to buy into the process.

You may even want to run an old system concurrently with a new system for several months to ensure that your staff accepts the new program and system and that the new system actually works as advertised. Again, the cost of running two systems may be small in comparison to a system failure or staff rebellion against the new system.

§ 8.03 What Accounts Receivable Technology Looks Like

For your perusal, I have included text and screen shots for each of two time and billing programs. You can get a sense of how this software would work and what sorts of reports you can run from the materials in Appendix I.

§ 8.04 Action Plan

- ◆ Think about the future needs of your firm before you research the available technology.
- ◆ Decide which reports your firm needs and be sure that all the programs you consider can produce these reports.
- ◆ Remember that your collections work is a process to be performed by you and other humans in your firm; technology is only a tool to assist you in the process.

The Collection Process

9

Out of debt, out of danger.

—Proverb

*A feast is made for laughter, and wine maketh merry;
but money answereth all things.*

—Ecclesiastes 10:19

CHAPTER CHECKLIST

- ◆ Overview
- ◆ Review the Terms of the Agreement
- ◆ Review the Local Rules of Professional Conduct
- ◆ Create a Written Policy
- ◆ Assigning Responsibility for Collections
- ◆ Accounts Receivable Reports
- ◆ Accounts Receivable Clerk
- ◆ Contacting the Client
- ◆ Obtaining the Information
- ◆ Discounting the Bill

§ 9.01 Overview

No matter how carefully you have worked to create a
good relationship with your clients, one of them is
going to be a collection problem. As I said from the

beginning, plan that each and every client will be a collection problem. That way, when the collection problem occurs, as it inevitably does, you will be well-armed with a variety of signed—and initialed—agreements.

In addition to having signed agreements, you will also want to be vigilant about how much time goes by before you begin trying to collect your bill. In collections, the more time that goes by, the harder the bill will be to collect. For example, when a bill is over 60 days past due, you will still be able to collect about 89 percent of the amount. However, that percentage drops to 67 percent after six months. At a year, the percentage you can expect to collect on the account is less than half: 45 percent.

§ 9.02 Review the Terms of the Agreement

Because you have asked your clients to sign and initial written agreements, the best possible way to begin the collection process is to review these agreements. In particular, the fee agreement should provide most of the information you will need to begin.

Be sure that you fully understand the terms of the client's agreement. You may be called upon to explain them to the person who will be collecting your past-due accounts. That person will be drafting a letter to the delinquent client explaining those terms.

§ 9.03 Review the Local Rules of Professional Conduct

Check the Rules of Professional Conduct in your local jurisdiction. As the *ABA Journal* has noted on several occasions, how you go about collecting the payment is as important as setting the price itself. See the ABA Model Rules of Professional Conduct, as well as a number of provisions in state and federal statutes.

Although you already have a signed fee agreement, you also want to be certain that you do not inadvertently do anything that would allow you to be censured for your conduct in the matter.

§ 9.04 Create a Written Policy

As I mentioned in the Overview to this chapter, it is of utmost importance that you move quickly to collect any overdue accounts. The more time you wait, the harder it will be to collect the bill. This conclusion is not only from my personal experience but also from the numerous publications put out by credit and collection professionals. Because you need to be able to move quickly, you need to create a written collections policy before you represent your first client. If that is not possible, create one as soon as you ask the client to sign the fee agreement. If the client does not pay your bill, you want to have everything in place to begin to collect immediately. Make this written policy and all accompanying forms, letters, and other documents part of your firm's collections handbook.

Your written policy must take into account two main functions: how to keep track of when clients are behind on their payments and how to contact clients when they are late with payments. The rest of this chapter deals with keeping track of late payments and setting up a collections department.

The main idea is to get on the problem early in order to keep your accounts receivable low and to keep your losses to a minimum. In addition, you want your staff to let you know quickly about clients who are not paying their bills so that you can immediately address the issue and, if necessary, stop working for those clients.

A complete collections policy includes everything that we have discussed so far. The firm's collections policy is everything from the beginning of the relationship with the client to the payment of the final bill. The best method is to have everything all together in one place. That way you can easily have copies made and give one to every lawyer in your firm. No collections policy can work until every single lawyer in the firm abides by its rules. Your collections policy should include:

◆ The firm's credit policy
◆ A sample client intake form
◆ A sample fee agreement
◆ A sample engagement letter
◆ Terms of collection

- ◆ A schedule of how the collection process works
- ◆ Samples of at least four kinds of collection letters
- ◆ Samples of letters to accompany telephone calls
- ◆ A copy of the form your collections manager uses when calling overdue accounts
- ◆ A list of the reports your collection manager runs every month to keep track of accounts receivable
- ◆ The firm's policy explaining what happens to lawyers who do not follow the firm's collections policy

Credit Policy

You created this earlier in Chapter 2. Include a copy of it here. It is important to have it written down. It has been said that a verbal contract isn't worth the paper it's written on and the same goes for your firm's credit policy. Write it down so that everyone in the firm knows what the firm's policy is.

Sample Client Forms

You cannot expect the lawyers in your firm to use the client forms unless you include copies in the collections policy. You will also want to make these available in computer templates so that support staff can just fill in the required information before asking clients to sign them. Remember, your firm needs to create a client-intake form, a fee agreement, and an engagement letter. If you require everyone in the firm to use the same forms, your problems with potential collections issues will drop considerably. You can find examples of all of these forms in the Appendix to this book.

Collection Terms

How behind do clients have to be on their accounts before the firm stops work? How late do clients have to be before the firm calls about their unpaid balances? How long do clients have before the firm sends their accounts to a collection agency? Your firm has to agree on these terms before you can put a collections policy into place. Later I will talk about the collection schedule, but the policy must come first.

As a firm, you must decide when a client becomes past due. Is it thirty days or sixty days after your bill has been sent? Once you determine this, then decide when you will begin to take action on the past-due account. When should someone call the client? At what stage does the firm stop work? Is it thirty days or sixty days after the bill is past due? Once you decide on these terms, you can construct a worthwhile schedule.

However, it is a good practice to write this up as a separate document and include it in the collection policy. In fact, you may want to include this information in your fee agreement with clients. You are just telling the client what to expect from you if he does not pay his bill on time. You are forming her expectations of how you will behave.

Collection Schedule

You can look in Appendix J to find a sample schedule. This document lists what sort of action happens on what day. In this example, the first call is made to the overdue account after forty-five days. In two-week increments after that, various letters are sent out that are followed up by more phone calls until finally the account is sent to a collection agency.

Collection Letters

There are four basic types of collection letters. Type 1 is a notice or reminder letter alerting the client to the past-due account. Type 2 is more of a customer-relations letter. It asks if there is any reason that the client has not paid the bill. Type 3 is more emphatic than Type 1 and insists that the bill be paid. Type 4 is the real consequence letter. It tells the client to pay by a specific date or the client's account will be sent to a collection agency. Examples of all four types are available in Appendix K of this book.

Collection letters have a definite place in the collection effort, but they do not work all by themselves. They work best in concert with telephone calls. The best success is obtained by employing the dial-and-smile method described later in this chapter and sending appropriate letters as necessary.

Letters to Accompany Telephone Calls

Appendix L has a variety of letters that can be used along with telephone calls. These include a letter to confirm the client's promise to pay, a letter to remind the client that the promised payment was not received, and a letter to thank the client for sending the promised payment. Used together with telephone calls and the series of four collection letters, these letters are a very effective method of getting payment from slow-paying clients.

Overdue Account Form and Monthly Reports

See the next section for the overdue account form as well as the types of monthly reports you may want to run to keep track of which clients have become delinquent on their bills.

Compliance Policy for Lawyers

The best-managed collection process will not work unless there is buy-in from every single lawyer in your firm. To do this, your firm needs a written policy that outlines what happens to lawyers who work for clients whose accounts are in arrears. The best possible approach includes both a "carrot" and a "stick." The carrot is an inducement, perhaps monetary, for the lawyer to follow the firm's collection policy. The stick is a punishment if the lawyer should fail to follow the policy. Your firm will never collect on past-due accounts if each partner gets to decide his or her own personal collections policy. For the good of the firm, and the firm's bottom line, there can be only one policy. You need to be sure that everyone is following it.

§ 9.05 Assigning Responsibility for Collections

You need to find someone on the financial side of your practice or firm who will be responsible for the entire collection process. If you are a solo practitioner or a small firm, you may have to hire a collections manager. The collection manager will be responsible for preparing the accounts receivable aging reports, contacting clients who have gone beyond the terms of their payment agreements, alerting lawyers to clients who have not paid, and monitoring the collection process from beginning to end. For more on this topic, see Chapter 27, "The Solo's Guide to Collecting Fees" in *Flying Solo: A Survival Guide for the Solo Lawyer,* Third Edition (ABA, 2001).

In the long run, it makes more sense to pay someone to handle this end of your business than to try to do the collections yourself. In my thirty-five years of experience, I have found that the collections process works much better if the lawyer delegates it to someone else. The lawyer should work with the client on the legal matters while the collections staff calls the client's accounting clerks or the clients themselves to clear up any problems with billings. The lawyer needs to discuss the payment issues up front with the client and then leave the business of collection to staff. Should the lawyer have to stop working for the client because of lack of payment, then the lawyer would discuss the withdrawal process with the client.

§ 9.06 Accounts Receivable Reports

AR Aging Report

There is an accounting form that may help you keep track of how much your clients owe and how late they are with their payments. This form can also provide an objective method to measure how well your collection process is working. It is called an aging report or aging analysis.

You prepare this report by listing the names of clients on the left side of the form and then dividing the rest of the form into columns with days late at the top. See the Aging Analysis form in Appendix M. This aging report can show you how old each client's billing is and how much each client owes you in consecutive 30-day billing cycles. The first column (0 to 30 days) is considered the "current" column. Bills in this column are not yet past due. Each column after that first one, however, represents another 30-day billing cycle during which you have not been paid. As soon as clients move to the 31-to-60–day column, your collections manager must alert you so that you can take appropriate action.

Another way to look at this information is to figure out what percentage of your outstanding bills fall into each 30-day period for each quarter of the year. See the Account Aging by Percentage by Quarter chart in Appendix N. If you look at your billings in this fashion at the end of each quarter, you will know exactly how well your collections process is working.

§ 9.07 Accounts Receivable Clerk

Working with your collections manager, you need to hire an accounts receivable clerk unless your practice is so small that the manager can do this as well as keep track of the entire collection process. Some lawyers attempt to save money by asking their support staff or assistants to do collection calls. This is a bad idea for two main reasons:

- ◆ the support staff person is identified with the lawyer, and
- ◆ the support staff person does not have the proper training.

You do not want the lawyer or anyone closely identified with the lawyer doing the collection calls. The client is used to talking with the lawyer about the matter at hand or issues of law. It can be very confusing for the client to have to talk with the lawyer about past-due bills as well as about the case at hand. This may become necessary if the client has ignored previous attempts by the firm to collect the bill and the lawyer is prepared to fire the client, or the lawyer is prepared to withdraw from the representation because the client has not paid for his services. Before this final break, the lawyer may want to attempt to talk to the client about the client's paying the bills.

Lawyers should do only two things: lawyering and marketing for new business. Everything else can be and should be done by someone else.

In addition, proper training in collections is absolutely necessary. There are laws governing how collection calls must be conducted, what can and cannot be said to clients who have not paid their bills, and how the client's privacy must be guarded by those doing the collection calls. It is a genuine cost savings to hire (even if only part-time) an accounts receivable clerk, a bookkeeper, or a collections manager to call clients about their past-due bills. You can easily tell if these people are doing their jobs by keeping track of your uncollected and aging past-due accounts.

§ 9.08 Contacting the Client

Call Sheets

Once you have determined who will contact clients, it is important to have this person keep good records and document every conversation with clients. Appendix O contains a sample call sheet to be filled out each time a client is contacted. Using this form will help your caller to keep meticulous track of the date and time of the call as well as who was called and what that person said. Recording this information will help the firm keep track of promises for payment as well as ensuring that clients are treated with respect.

Dial and Smile

One process that I suggest to find out what clients are really saying if they are not paying the bill is called Dial and Smile. See Appendix P for a sample script of this technique. A flowchart of this process is provided in Figure 2.

- ◆ First, have your accounts receivable clerk or your collections manager call the client. The caller should smile before dialing the phone number—and remain smiling and friendly throughout the entire phone conversation. Confirm that the client or authorized person for making payment is the person speaking on the other end of the line.
- ◆ Have the caller ask the client if he or she *received* the statement. If the answer is no, fax, deliver by messenger, or send a copy of the statement to the client immediately.
- ◆ If the client says, "No, there is no problem with the bill," then ask the next question: "When can *we expect to receive payment* in our office?" (not "When will the check be mailed?").
- ◆ Normally, the client will make a commitment for a payment—often only a partial one. Have the clerk mark the calendar for that date. Have the clerk attempt to get a commitment of no further than ten days out.
- ◆ If the check does not arrive on time, have the clerk call the client on the *very next day* and go through the same set of questions. Each set of calls should be approximately *ten days apart*. Complete this process several times over a period of not more than six to eight weeks.

After this time, if the bill is not paid or at least reduced substantially, you must decide whether to continue working for the client or terminate the lawyer-client relationship, and then whether to sue for fees earned to date but not paid.

Figure 2
Flowchart of Dial-and-Smile Process

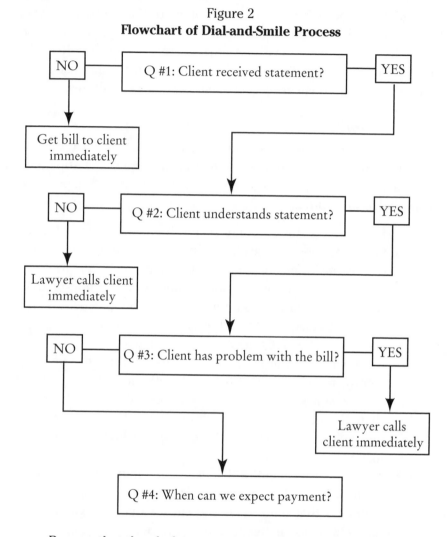

Be sure that the clerk is recording the client's responses in the file. This will build a record that no complaint was ever registered by the client or that every complaint was addressed to the client's satisfaction if ever you should have to sue the client to collect fees or if the client, at some future date, were to bring a case for malpractice.

The clerk should always be friendly and smiling on the telephone (hence the term "dial and smile"). The caller should under no circumstances be accusatory or in any way hostile to the client, even if the client fails to honor one or more commitments for the payment of money due.

Calls and Letters in Tandem

When the client promises to pay a certain amount, send a letter confirming that agreement. If the client sends the payment as expected, send the payment-received letter. If the client does not send the payment as expected, send the missed-payment letter. A suggested order and timetable of both letters and calls is included in Appendix J in the collection schedule.

Whatever letters you decide to use in your collection effort, be sure to use the letters in tandem with telephone calls. Letters alone do not work because they are too easy to throw away and forget about. A person who follows up on every promise the client makes is much more effective. The value of the phone calls is that the caller telephones the client the next day after the client has failed to live up to a promise. This call reminds the client about the past-due account. Like a very polite bulldog, your caller can continue to remind the client until the client pays the bill in full or you and the firm decide to send the client's billing to a collection agency.

§ 9.09 Obtaining the Information

The great advantage of the dial-and-smile method is that you will find out if the client has not paid because of a dispute about the bill. The client has an opportunity to explain if there is some confusion over the bill or if the bill contains errors. Obviously, any errors should be corrected immediately and a new bill should be faxed or sent via messenger to the client as soon as possible. If the bill is not clear or the client does not understand it, then the lawyer can call and discuss it with the client.

With the first call, your clerk should be able to tell you which nonpayments were based on confusion or mistakes and which were signals of a collection problem. After any confusion has been cleared up, you need to find out whether or not your client is unable to pay or if the client disputes the bill.

In the case of the client being unable to pay, there are a variety of things that you can do to resolve the matter quickly. First and foremost, do not do any more work for a client who is unable to pay. Second, consider changing from an hourly to a percentage basis, depending on the matter you are handling for the client. Third, walk away. Write the billing off. In the long run, you will lose less because you will not be paying the collections staff to keep calling a client who will never be able to pay. In addition, you are much less likely to be sued for malpractice if you walk away from the situation.

Disputes with clients can be difficult to resolve. Nonetheless, it is best to resolve these issues between the lawyer and the client as soon as possible. Many disputes are caused by clients complaining about overbilling. These clients suggest that the time the lawyer worked was unnecessary, that the representation of the lawyer was ineffective, or that the work was excessive and done without the client's consent.

You can escape most of these complaints by following my earlier advice about getting the client's approval in writing before you take any action. However, if you are still in the middle of such a dispute, ask the client what he or she would like you to do to resolve it. It may involve cutting your fee. Listen carefully to the suggestion. Be sure to check your emotion (anger; hurt by the client's failure to appreciate your good work) at the door. This requires a business decision based on your best financial and professional interests.

§ 9.10 Discounting the Bill

Generally, price is not the issue with clients. Therefore, I suggest that lawyers do not discount their fees after the fee agreement has been signed. However, in a collection situation, it is important to do whatever is necessary to resolve the conflict.

Clients who argue about overbilling are often just angling for a discount to your bill. If, after all your work to communicate with the client, the client is merely interested in a fee discount, give it. Do it to get rid of the matter and the client.

Do not work for the client in the future. Under no circumstances do you want clients to think that they can cut your price or fee after they have already agreed to pay you the full amount. This sort of price shenanigans is quite popular during the month of December with clients of large law firms. Clients agree to pay their large bills in order to wangle huge discounts because the remuneration system for partners is based upon how much has been collected by the end of the year. Any bills collected in January do not count for another eleven months. Some of these clients have gotten into the habit of attempting to discount their lawyers' fees for every matter.

§ 9.11 Action Plan

- ◆ Create a written collection policy.
- ◆ Select someone from the financial side to call clients and monitor the collection policy.
- ◆ Create and monitor accounts receivable reports.
- ◆ Educate accounts receivable clerks to keep meticulous records of their conversations with clients.
- ◆ Discount your fees only if it is the only way to settle a dispute with a client and get paid.

When In-House Collection Fails | 10

Money, it turned out, was exactly like sex; you thought of nothing else if you didn't have it and thought of other things if you did.

—James Baldwin

There are few ways in which a man can be more innocently employed than in getting money.

—Samuel Johnson

CHAPTER CHECKLIST
- Cutting Your Losses
- Efforts from the Firm
- Collection Agencies
- Filing Suit
- Winning

§ 10.01 Cutting Your Losses

If you have tried consistently to collect on a past-due bill for a year and you haven't gotten even a partial payment, it is time to cut your losses. Consider the administrative time and expense that you have already spent to try and collect this account. Do you want to spend still more money to collect a small percentage of what you are owed?

Include a section on cutting your losses in your collection handbook. Decide how much time (which is money any way you look at it) you or the firm will spend to collect accounts before you count the bill as a loss, send the bill to a collection agency, or sue the client in court. Obviously, clients who do not have the money should be written off as soon as you are certain that the client is actually unable to pay your bill and is not merely placing you at the bottom of his or her priority list. The other two options are covered in the rest of this chapter.

§ 10.02 Efforts from the Firm

Discuss the situation with the person in charge of your collection efforts. What are your chances of getting your fees paid? If the client has paid some of what is owed, consider working with the client through the good offices of your in-house collection staff. If the client has not made even a partial payment and is still fiscally sound, you need to consider your other two options.

§ 10.03 Collection Agencies

Collection agencies have the staff and the skill to get at least a portion of your bill paid. However, they do come with a few problems of their own. For one, collection agencies will take a percentage of everything they collect. While you may be able to negotiate a fee as low as 25 percent of what is owed, sometimes this figure can rise to 50 percent on older bills. Another problem is that you will be judged by the behavior of your collection agency. Check with your local jurisdiction to see if there are any possible liabilities to consider with respect to the Rules of Professional Conduct.

Before you take this step, carefully check the appropriate files to be sure that they are clean and contain no evidence—actual or perceived—of malpractice. Then notify the client(s) that you intend to send their fee bill to a collection agency. Send them a letter explaining what you are doing and why you are doing it. Give your clients a week's notice and then pass them along to the collection agency. For Collection Letter 4, see Appendix K at the back of this book.

If you and your in-house collection staff have done your job, you will have to send only a few, if any, accounts to a collection agency.

§ 10.04 Filing Suit

If the amount you are owed warrants it, you may also want to consider the last possible option: suing your client for fees. Before you make this final decision, there are a few considerations.

Required Activities

Review your local Rules of Professional Conduct for required activities such as arbitration or mediation before filing suit. What other courses of action do your Rules suggest or require before you sue your client?

Insurance Company

Check with your insurance carrier to review any concerns that they have about the issue. Read the fine print on your policy to make sure that you will not void any coverage by taking a client to court. Remember, the advice of every carrier is to write-off the account and not sue. That is not my advice—if all the steps and precautions outlined in this book are taken.

Review the Statute of Limitations

You may want to wait for one year to avoid a cross-complaint for negligence. Sue under the contract clause. The client will likely make an offsetting claim, but no affirmative award is generally available. Prepare your case, including appropriate declarations, and seek a prejudgment remedy. Note that some states are changing their period of filing a lawsuit under their statute of limitations from one year to two years.

Review Your File

The larger the balance owed to the law firm, the more important it is to review the file before deciding to file a lawsuit against a client. Your review must result in believing that there was no error, no inadvertent omission, and no negligence by the responsible lawyers in the law firm. In other words, the file is clean and can withstand scrutiny by an independent third party.

§ 10.05 Winning

Lawyers have the right to be paid in accordance with signed agreements and in conformity with the Rules of Professional Conduct. If you have adhered to your side of the agreement and done what you said you would do, then the client should do the same.

While the prevailing wisdom at this time is not to sue, I have heard from a wide variety of my colleagues who routinely sue and just as routinely win. If you have followed my advice and documented everything from the very beginning, you should be in a good position to win your case.

§ 10.06 Action Plan

- ◆ Make sure to include a post-collections section in your collection handbook.
- ◆ Write off clients who are unable to pay you.
- ◆ Continue to use your in-house staff to collect from clients who have made partial payments.
- ◆ Consider going to a collection agency for those clients who have not made even a partial payment.
- ◆ If the balance is large enough, consider taking your client to court for nonpayment.

Final Words 11

> *. . . and they give you cash, which is just as good as money.*
>
> —Yogi Berra,
> television commercial

> *Check enclosed.*
>
> —Dorothy Parker

CHAPTER CHECKLIST
- Benefits from a Better Collections Process
- Merchant Account
- Collaborative Relationships with the Accounts-Payable Department
- Knowing Others in the Client's Organization

§ 11.01 Benefits from a Better Collection Process

Understanding the credit process, the growth of accounts receivable in the sales/revenue cycle, and the need to have an effective collection process in place will add to the success of the law firm. Controlling and reducing the DSO, or days sales outstanding, increases the firm's cash flow by many thousands of dollars and further enhances the firm's financial strength.

§ 11.02 Merchant Account

In today's world, even businesses use credit cards to pay their professional services. Establishing a merchant account may be another way for the law firm to assist its collection efforts. Offering the client the option of setting up automatic payment by way of the client's credit card should be considered by the lawyer. It is usually easy and inexpensive to create a merchant account. Not every client will accept this, but enough do to make the effort and expense worthwhile. Reduction of the DSO is money in the lawyer's pocket and is almost as good as cash in advance. Special note: If you use a merchant account, reviewing the bank's policies will prevent a charge-back later if the client subsequently objects. To avoid confusion later, state in the engagement letter or fee letter that payments made by credit card are nonrefundable.

§ 11.03 Collaborative Relationships with the Accounts-Payable Department

Collaborative relationships produce the best results for everyone, both the client and the vendor-lawyer. This is becoming better understood in terms of the attorney-client relationship. What is yet to be understood is that a collaborative relationship between the lawyer and the client's accounts payable department is also important. In one instance, for example, the client's accounts payable department wanted to ensure that the vendor would be able to handle the needs of the client. So, the accounts payable manager instructed the vendor to raise his price to the client and offer a cash discount for payment within ten days of billing. By having an advocate for the vendor within the client's payable department, the client was assured of having its needs met and the vendor was assured of prompt payment.

§ 11.04 Knowing Others in the Client's Organization

Another rule of thumb is to know as many people within the client's organization as possible. Just days before filing Chapter 11, a client gave to a vendor payment of an outstanding receivable. The result of this "favored treatment" was to almost completely pay off the outstanding account receivable; the vendor was not himself placed on the verge of bankruptcy by virtue of the client's financial challenges. This payment was made because of the close relationship between the parties and the collaborative nature of their previous dealings.

These are examples of the importance of collaborative relationships to lawyers, as well as other vendors, with the people who pay the bills for the client.

§ 11.05 Conclusion

Some law firms appear to be successful to the eyes of outsiders. In one such case, the members of the firm still thought they needed some marketing punch—some pizzazz that would increase their client base and their gross revenue. They retained a marketing consultant to help them with this project. The marketing consultant dutifully interviewed the members of the firm, checked out the reputation of the firm in its marketplace, and thought that something was not right.

The problem was not a question of the marketplace. It was not a question of the reputation of the firm, and it was not even a question of the firm's ability to attract new clients. All of these factors seemed positive. But the consultant felt something was wrong under the surface, and she could not quite put her finger on what it was. She called me.

As it turned out, one of the threshold issues for the firm was that it was billing $1 and collecting only 68 cents on that dollar, but no one realized this. Their controls were inadequate to bring this to the attention of the partners with enough force that they would address the issue.

One of my goals in this book has been to provide a framework around which to structure your collection efforts. The marketplace knows you are a valuable resource. Your client in need will know how much value you provide to him or her. However, there is no reason to work hard in performing services your client wants and needs only to find out that the agreement with your client works in just one direction: You do the work, and the client fails to pay you. Not only is that arrangement unfair, it is also unwise, to say the least.

Lawyering is a two-way agreement—a contract, a partnership. You do the work, and you are entitled to receive the benefit for which you bargained. If you are an employee for a public-service entity, you know that you will receive thanks and a paycheck on payday. There is no reason to permit your client to change the agreement after the fact just because you are a private practitioner.

All three parts are integral to operating a business: First, getting the client (and keeping the client happy by exceeding expectations); second, doing the work (operating efficiently and effectively); and third, getting paid. Following the rules in this book will allow you to close the circle in this business cycle and permit you to start the cycle again in new matters with satisfied clients who continue to bring you an ever-increasing market share of their legal work and refer more of their colleagues and friends to you.

Appendices

Appendix A
NEW CLIENT INTAKE FORM—SAMPLE 1

Date _____

Full Legal Name of Firm: _____

Street Address: _____

City: _____ State: _____ ZIP Code: _____

Full Name and Address of Owner(s) or authorized corporate official

_____

_____

Federal Tax ID # or SSN: _____

Driver's License Number: _____

Reason for Leaving Last Law Firm:

_____

_____

Type of Company:

❐ Proprietorship   ❐ Partnership   ❐ Corporation

Age of Company: _____ State of Incorporation: _____

Contacts:

Name of Contact for Credit and Collections:

_____

Telephone Number: _____ Email: _____

Name of Contact for Check Authorization:

_____

Telephone Number: _____ Email: _____

Trade References:

Name	Title	Telephone
Name	Title	Telephone
Name	Title	Telephone

Bank References:

Name   Street   State and ZIP Code

Name of Bank Official Responsible for Account:

_____ Telephone Number: _____

Applicant's signature attests financial responsibility, ability, and willingness to pay our invoices in accordance with the following terms.

[List terms of payment. See text for further discussion.]

Firm Name _____

By _____ Title _____

By _____ Title _____

NEW CLIENT INTAKE FORM—SAMPLE 2

Client Information	
Client Number:	
Client Name and Contact Information:	

Business Information	
Business Name and Address:	
Business Description:	

Matter Information	
Matter Number:	
Matter Name:	
Amount Involved:	
Matter Type:	
Matter Description:	

Type of Services to be Performed:	

Other Information:	

Why Matter Should Be Approved:	

Lawyer Information

Client Lawyer:	
Billing Lawyer:	
Responsible Lawyer:	
Working Lawyer:	
Source Credit:	
Referral Source Description:	

Client Legal History:	
Previous Lawyer:	
Current Lawyer:	

Conflicts Information

Names of All Parties, Witnesses, Experts, et al.:	
Relationships:	
Status: Conflicts do/do not exist; waived	

Financial Information	
Hourly Billing Rate:	
Alt. Fee Type:	
Fee Estimated; Fee Discussed (date):	

Trade References:	Name	Title	Telephone
Reference #1			
Reference #2			
Reference #3			

Bank References	
Name:	
Address:	
Name of Responsible Bank Officer:	
Telephone Number:	

Address Information	
Client Name:	
Attention:	
Address:	
Telephone:	
Facsimile:	

Attachments	
Proposed Engagement Letter:	
Proposed Disclosure Letter:	
Pre-Intake Conflict Checklist:	
Contingency Letter:	
Other:	

Accounts Receivable	
Total AR:	
0–30:	
31–60:	
61–90:	
91–121:	
Unbilled:	

Commonly Used Financial Ratios
During the Intake Process

Category	Ratio
Operating performance	EBITA/Sales (Earnings before income taxes/sales)
	Net income/Sales
	Net income/Net worth
	Net income/Total assets
	Sales/Fixed assets
Debt service coverage	EBITA/interest
	Free cash flow
Financial leverage	Long-term debt/capitalization
	Long-term debt/tangible net worth
	Current liabilities/tangible net worth
Liquidity	Current ratio (Current assets/current liabilities)
	Quick ratio (Cash + accounts receivable/current liabilities)
	Inventory/Net sales

Appendix B
RETAINERS: ISSUES CHECKLIST

❏ *Amount of retainer*
The engagement agreement must set forth the retainer amount. An explanation regarding the type of account in which the retainer will be deposited is also warranted.

❏ *Refundable or nonrefundable*
The engagement agreement must disclose whether the retainer is refundable and, if so, when any residual amount will be refunded to the client. If the retainer is nonrefundable, it must be a reasonable amount.

❏ *Interest or noninterest bearing*
Engagement agreements should indicate whether the accounts in which the retainers are deposited are interest bearing and, if so, who will collect such interest. IOLTA interest provisions are of particular importance.

❏ *Replenishment requirements*
If the law firm requires replenishment of the retainer or a minimum balance, these terms must be set forth in the engagement agreement. If the firm reserves the right to demand replenishment, then perhaps an adequate notice period to the client would be preferred, rather than replenishment upon demand.

❏ *Application of retainer to fees and/or costs*
The engagement agreement should disclose whether the retainer will be applied to fees, costs, or both, and should also disclose how the billings will reflect depletion of the retainer for such payments.

❏ *Timing of retainer application*
If the retainer is characterized as a security interest for regular payment of fees and/or costs, then the retainer terms should reflect under what circumstances the retainer may be invaded.

ENGAGEMENT AGREEMENTS/NONENGAGEMENT LETTERS: ISSUES CHECKLIST

Engagement Agreements

❏ Client and attorney identity

❏ Conflict of interest and attorney-client privilege issues

❏ Scope of service

❏ Responsibilities of attorney and client

❏ Chronology of events

❏ Fee arrangement

❏ Payment of costs and disbursements

❏ Billing format, cycle, and payment expectations, including interest

❏ Retainer terms

❏ Delegation of work assignments

❏ Rate changes

❏ Withdrawal

❏ Arbitration provisions

❏ Binding provisions

❏ Execution by attorney and client

Nonengagement Letters

❏ Declination of Representation

❏ Statutes of Limitation and Other Time Sensitive Dates

❏ Duty to Seek Other Counsel

❏ Conflicts of Interest

FILE-OPENING CHECKLIST

Pre-Opening Procedures

- ❏ Client screening conducted
- ❏ Conflict of interest checks performed and potential conflicts analyzed
- ❏ Sufficient client information gathered
- ❏ Statutes of limitation and other time-sensitive dates identified and entered into the docket system
- ❏ Engagement agreements of scope of service letters utilized
- ❏ Retainers collected

New Client/Matter Form Requirements

- ❏ Client information
- ❏ Conflicts information
- ❏ Time-sensitive dates
- ❏ Fee/billing information
- ❏ Administrative information
- ❏ Verifications of docket entry and conflicts check and data entry
- ❏ Verification of review by billing partner/department head/ managing partner

Appendix C
SAMPLE FEE AGREEMENT 1

Date:

Joseph Client
1234 Alphabet Way
Anytown, New York 20034

This letter will confirm our understanding that, upon your signature, you have retained (name of your law firm) to represent you in connection with (describe matter).

Before proceeding with this legal work, the firm requires a deposit and initial retainer of $_____.

Our fees are based on hourly rates for the services of lawyers in our firm. Attached to this letter is a listing of lawyers who may work on your matter and their corresponding current rates. Charges are made for all professional services connected with your matter, including in-person and telephone conferences. In addition to fees for professional services, the firm bills for out-of-pocket expenses we incur including, but not limited to, long distance telephone charges, photocopying costs, postage, mileage in accordance with current Internal Revenue Service standards, filing and recording fees, etc.

Our bills are normally prepared and mailed within a few days of the beginning of each month. All bills are due and payable upon receipt.

If bills are not paid when due, the firm reserves the right to discontinue legal services and to withdraw from representing you as a client. However, we will not discontinue service without giving you notice of our intention. In the event of the firm's withdrawal, we will mail a certified letter to your last known address. Upon receipt of your written request and payment of any necessary shipping costs, all your papers and property in the firm's possession will be returned to you.

We look forward to working with you.

Sincerely yours,

_____

(Law Firm by Lawyer in charge of client relationship)

Agreement and Acceptance:

I agree to the above terms and conditions.

_____

_____

(Client)

Dated: _____

SAMPLE FEE AGREEMENT 2

Date:
Joseph Client
1234 Alphabet Way
Anytown, New York 20034

Attorney-Client Fee Contract
This attorney-client fee contract ("Contract") is entered into by and
between Joseph Client ("Client") and (name of law firm) ("Lawyer").

♦ CONDITIONS
This Contract will not take effect, and Lawyer will have no obligations
to provide legal services, until Client returns a signed copy of this
Contract and pays the initial deposit called for under paragraph 3.

♦ SCOPE AND DUTIES
Client hires lawyer to provide legal services in connection with
(state description of matter). Lawyer shall provide those legal services reasonably required to represent Client, and shall take all reasonable steps necessary to keep Client informed of progress and to
respond to Client's inquiries. Client shall be truthful with Lawyer,
cooperate with Lawyer, keep Lawyer informed of developments,
abide by this Contract, pay Lawyer's fees as set forth in monthly
billing statements on time and keep Lawyer advised of Client's current address, telephone number, and other contact information.

♦ DEPOSIT
Client shall deposit $____ by _____. The sum will be deposited
in a trust account, to be used to pay:

(Client to initial appropriate line)
a.   Costs and expenses only _____

b.   Costs and expenses and fees for legal services _____

Client hereby authorizes Lawyer to withdraw sums from the trust
account to pay the costs and/or fees Client incurs as initialed above.

Any unused deposit at the conclusion of Lawyer's services will be refunded.

◆ LEGAL FEES

Client agrees to pay for legal services at the following rates:

Partners	$____ hour
Associates	$____ hour
Paralegals	$____ hour
Law clerks	$____ hour

and for other personnel as follows:

Lawyer charges in minimum units of one-tenth (1/10th) of an hour.

◆ COSTS AND EXPENSES

In addition to paying legal fees, Client shall reimburse Lawyer for all costs and expenses incurred by Lawyer, including, but not limited to, process servers' fees, fees fixed by law or assessed by courts or other agencies, court reporters' fees, long distance telephone calls, messenger and other delivery fees, postage, in-office photocopying at $___ per page, parking, mileage at $___ per mile, investigation expenses, consultants' fees, expert witness fees and other similar items. Client authorizes Lawyer to incur all reasonable costs and to hire any investigators, consultants, or expert witnesses reasonably necessary in Lawyer's judgment, unless one or both of the clauses below are initialed by Client and Lawyer.

___ Lawyer shall obtain Client's consent before incurring any cost in excess of $ ___.

___ Lawyer shall obtain Client's consent before retaining outside investigators, consultants, or expert witnesses.

◆ STATEMENTS

Lawyer shall send Client periodic statements for fees and cost incurred. Client shall pay Lawyer's statements within _____days after each statement's date. Client may request a statement at intervals of no less than 30 days. Upon Client's request, Lawyer will provide a statement within 10 days.

◆   LIEN

Client hereby grants Lawyer a lien on any and all claims or causes of action that are the subject of Lawyer's representation under this Contract. Lawyer's lien will be for any sums due and owing to Lawyer at the conclusion of Lawyer's services. The lien will attach to any recovery Client may obtain, whether by arbitration award, judgment, settlement, or otherwise.

◆   DISCHARGE AND WITHDRAWAL

Client may discharge Lawyer at any time. Lawyer may withdraw with Client's consent or for good cause. Good cause includes Client's breach of this Contract (including failure to pay lawyer's fee timely), Client's refusal to cooperate with Lawyer or to follow Lawyer's advice on a material matter or any other fact or circumstance that would render Lawyer's continuing representation unlawful or unethical.

◆   CONCLUSION OF SERVICES

When Lawyer's services conclude, all unpaid charges shall become immediately due and payable. After Lawyer's services conclude, Lawyer will, upon Client's request and payment of shipment cost, deliver Client's file to Client, along with any Client funds or property in Lawyer's possession.

◆   DISCLAIMER OF GUARANTEE

Nothing in this Contract and nothing in Lawyer's statements to Client will be construed as a promise or guarantee about the outcome of Client's matter. Lawyer makes no such promises or guarantees. Lawyer's comments about the outcome of Client's matter are an expression of opinion only.

◆   EFFECTIVE DATE

This Contract will take effect when Client has performed the conditions stated in paragraph 1, but its effective date will be retroactive to the date Lawyer first provided services. The date at the beginning of this Contract is for reference only. Even if this Contract does not take effect, Client will be obligated to pay Lawyer for the reasonable value of any services Lawyer may have performed for Client.

Name of Lawyer

By: _____

Name of Client

By: _____

Client Address _____

_____

Client Telephone Number _____

Client Fax Number _____

Client Email address _____

Appendix D
STATUS REPORT—SAMPLE 1

JOSEPH J. LAWYER Attorney at Law 123 Alphabet Way Anytown, USA 12345	❏ SPECIAL ❏ MONTHLY ❏ QUARTERLY ❏ SEMIANNUAL ❏ ANNUAL	**STATUS REPORT**	CLIENT:
			MATTER:
			FILE NO.:

TYPE OF CASE AND GENERAL PROGRESS OF MATTER:

OFFICE	GENERAL LITIGATION	ESTATE
❏ Case Evaluation	❏ Case Evaluation	❏ Filing Petition

❏ Research and
  Investigation
	❏ Research and
	  Investigation
		❏ Assembling
		  Assets

❏ Negotiation	❏ Pleading	❏ Preparing Inventory

❏ Document
  Drafting
	❏ Discovery	❏ Dealing with
		  Claims

❏ Closing	❏ Motions and
	  Pre-Trial
		❏ Filing and
		  Paying Taxes

	❏ Final Trial
	  Preparation
		❏ Preparing
		  Final Account

	❏ Trial	❏ Distribution and Closing
	❏ Post-Trial (Or Appeal)	

CURRENT STATUS:

I am currently waiting for the following items: To be provided by: ❏ _____ ❏ You _____ ❏ _____ ❏ You _____ ❏ _____ ❏ You _____ ❏ _____ ❏ You _____	My next efforts on your behalf will be:

ACCOUNT STATUS:

The status of your account is presently:
- ❏ Current. **THANK YOU.**
- ❏ In arrears _____ months in the amount of $_____.
- ❏ Please remit or make arrangements to settle this account.
- ❏ We need a further deposit of $_____ into your
  Trust Account.

OTHER NOTES:

Thank you,

Dated:_____, _____

_____
Joseph J. Lawyer

STATUS REPORT—SAMPLE 2

Matter: _____

Client: _____

Responsible Lawyer: _____

Date of Invoice: _____; Date invoice received: _____

Billing Lawyer: _____

Matter Number/Agreement Number: _____

__ 1.

Billings	Fees	Disbursements	Total
Invoice month:			
Year to date:			
Project to date:			

__ 2. Effect of current invoice on budget:
    Within Project Budget? ___ Yes ___ No
    Within Annual Budget? ___ Yes ___ No

__ 3. Anticipated billings for next two months:
    Amount $ _____ and $ _____
    Consistent with case planned and last status
    report? ___ Yes ___ No

__ 4. Any developments that call for review of the project case plan
    or indicate the need to revise the Project Budget?
        ___ Yes ___ No

__ 5. Date of last status report: _____

__ 6. Current matter status:
        __ Evaluation
        __ Research and investigation
        __ Negotiation
        __ Document drafting
        __ Pleadings drafting
        __ Discovery
        __ Trial preparation

__ 7. Currently waiting for the following items or actions:

	Items	*To be provided by whom*
a.	_____	_____
b.	_____	_____
c.	_____	_____

Appendix E
CASE/MATTER BUDGET

Case/Matter Plan and Budget
2003

	Jan.	Feb.	Mar.	April
Evaluation				
Research and Investigation				
Negotiation				
Document Drafting				
Pleadings Drafting				
Discovery (Note: See worksheet below)				
Trial Preparation				
Trial				

Case/Matter Plan and Budget—Discovery
2003

	Jan.	Feb.	Mar.	April
Strategy and Analysis				
Document Production				
Interrogatories				
Depositions				
Motion for Summary Judgment				

LITIGATION BUDGET

Litigation Plan and Budget—2003

Activity	1st Quarter	2nd Quarter	3rd Quarter	4th Quarter

Litigation Budget Worksheet:
Case Assessment, Development, and Administration

	Estimated Hours	Estimated Average Hourly Rate	Estimated Total Amount
Analysis Strategy			
Experts/Consultants			
Document/File Management			

(continued on next page)

	Estimated Hours	Estimated Average Hourly Rate	Estimated Total Amount
Budgeting			
Settlement/Nonbinding ADR			
Client Reports			
Pretrial Pleadings and Motions			
Preliminary Injunctions/ Provisional Remedies			
Court-Mandated Conferences			
Written Motions			
Written Discovery			
Document Discovery			
Depositions			
Expert Discovery			
Discovery Motions			
Other Discovery			
Trial Preparations			
Trial			
Post-Trial Motions			
Enforcement Proceedings			

Appendix F
ABA MODEL RULES

ABA Model Rule of Professional Conduct 1.5 reprinted from Model Rules of Professional Conduct, 2003 Edition, *published by the Center for Professional Responsibility, American Bar Association, 2003. Reprinted with permission.* Copies of ABA Model Rules of Professional Conduct *2003 are available from Service Center, American Bar Association, 750 N. Lake Shore Drive, Chicago, IL 60611-4497, 1-800-285-2221.*

RULE 1.5: FEES

(a)   A lawyer shall not make an agreement for, charge, or collect an unreasonable fee or an unreasonable amount for expenses. The factors to be considered in determining the reasonableness of a fee include the following:

(1)   the time and labor required, the novelty and difficulty of the questions involved, and the skill requisite to perform the legal service properly;

(2)   the likelihood, if apparent to the client, that the acceptance of the particular employment will preclude other employment by the lawyer;

(3)   the fee customarily charged in the locality for similar legal services;

(4)   the amount involved and the results obtained;

(5)   the time limitations imposed by the client or by the circumstances;

(6)   the nature and length of the professional relationship with the client;

(7)   the experience, reputation, and ability of the lawyer or lawyers performing the services; and

(8)   whether the fee is fixed or contingent.

(b)   The scope of the representation and the basis or rate of the fee and expenses for which the client will be responsible shall be communicated to the client, preferably in writing, before or within a reasonable time after commencing the representation, except when the lawyer will charge a regularly represented client on the same basis or rate. Any changes in the basis or rate of the fee or expenses shall also be communicated to the client.

(c)   A fee may be contingent on the outcome of the matter for which the service is rendered, except in a matter in which a contingent fee is prohibited by paragraph (d) or other law. A contingent fee agreement shall be in a writing signed by the client and shall state the method by which the fee is to be determined, including the percentage or percentages that shall accrue to the lawyer in the event of settlement, trial or appeal; litigation and other expenses to be deducted from the recovery; and whether such expenses are to be deducted before or after the contingent fee is calculated. The agreement must clearly notify the client of any expenses for which the client will be liable whether or not the client is the prevailing party. Upon conclusion of a contingent fee matter, the lawyer shall provide the client with a written statement stating the outcome of the matter and, if there is a recovery, showing the remittance to the client and the method of its determination.

(d)   A lawyer shall not enter into an arrangement for, charge, or collect:

(1)   any fee in a domestic relations matter, the payment or amount of which is contingent upon the securing of a divorce or upon the amount of alimony or support, or property settlement in lieu thereof; or

(2)   a contingent fee for representing a defendant in a criminal case.

(e)   A division of a fee between lawyers who are not in the same firm may be made only if:

(1)   the division is in proportion to the services performed by each lawyer or each lawyer assumes joint responsibility for the representation;

(2)   the client agrees to the arrangement, including the share each lawyer will receive, and the agreement is confirmed in writing; and

(3)   the total fee is reasonable.

Comment

Reasonableness of Fee and Expenses

[1]   Paragraph (a) requires that lawyers charge fees that are reasonable under the circumstances. The factors specified in (1) through (8) are not exclusive. Nor will each factor be relevant in each instance. Paragraph (a) also requires that expenses for which

the client will be charged must be reasonable. A lawyer may seek reimbursement for the cost of services performed in-house, such as copying, or for other expenses incurred in-house, such as telephone charges, either by charging a reasonable amount to which the client has agreed in advance or by charging an amount that reasonably reflects the cost incurred by the lawyer.

Basis or Rate of Fee

[2]   When the lawyer has regularly represented a client, they ordinarily will have evolved an understanding concerning the basis or rate of the fee and the expenses for which the client will be responsible. In a new client-lawyer relationship, however, an understanding as to fees and expenses must be promptly established. Generally, it is desirable to furnish the client with at least a simple memorandum or copy of the lawyer's customary fee arrangements that states the general nature of the legal services to be provided, the basis, rate or total amount of the fee and whether and to what extent the client will be responsible for any costs, expenses or disbursements in the course of the representation. A written statement concerning the terms of the engagement reduces the possibility of misunderstanding.

[3]   Contingent fees, like any other fees, are subject to the reasonableness standard of paragraph (a) of this Rule. In determining whether a particular contingent fee is reasonable, or whether it is reasonable to charge any form of contingent fee, a lawyer must consider the factors that are relevant under the circumstances. Applicable law may impose limitations on contingent fees, such as a ceiling on the percentage allowable, or may require a lawyer to offer clients an alternative basis for the fee. Applicable law also may apply to situations other than a contingent fee, for example, government regulations regarding fees in certain tax matters.

Terms of Payment

[4]   A lawyer may require advance payment of a fee, but is obliged to return any unearned portion. See Rule 1.16(d). A lawyer may accept property in payment for services, such as an ownership interest in an enterprise, providing this does not involve acquisition of a proprietary interest in the cause of action or subject matter of the litigation contrary to Rule 1.8 (i). However, a fee

paid in property instead of money may be subject to the requirements of Rule 1.8(a) because such fees often have the essential qualities of a business transaction with the client.

[5]   An agreement may not be made whose terms might induce the lawyer improperly to curtail services for the client or perform them in a way contrary to the client's interest. For example, a lawyer should not enter into an agreement whereby services are to be provided only up to a stated amount when it is foreseeable that more extensive services probably will be required, unless the situation is adequately explained to the client. Otherwise, the client might have to bargain for further assistance in the midst of a proceeding or transaction. However, it is proper to define the extent of services in light of the client's ability to pay. A lawyer should not exploit a fee arrangement based primarily on hourly charges by using wasteful procedures.

Prohibited Contingent Fees

[6]   Paragraph (d) prohibits a lawyer from charging a contingent fee in a domestic relations matter when payment is contingent upon the securing of a divorce or upon the amount of alimony or support or property settlement to be obtained. This provision does not preclude a contract for a contingent fee for legal representation in connection with the recovery of postjudgment balances due under support, alimony or other financial orders because such contracts do not implicate the same policy concerns.

Division of Fee

[7]   A division of fee is a single billing to a client covering the fee of two or more lawyers who are not in the same firm. A division of fee facilitates association of more than one lawyer in a matter in which neither alone could serve the client as well, and most often is used when the fee is contingent and the division is between a referring lawyer and a trial specialist. Paragraph (e) permits the lawyers to divide a fee either on the basis of the proportion of services they render or if each lawyer assumes responsibility for the representation as a whole. In addition, the client must agree to the arrangement, including the share that each lawyer is to receive, and the agreement must be confirmed in writing. Contingent fee

agreements must be in a writing signed by the client and must otherwise comply with paragraph (c) of this Rule. Joint responsibility for the representation entails financial and ethical responsibility for the representation as if the lawyers were associated in a partnership. A lawyer should only refer a matter to a lawyer whom the referring lawyer reasonably believes is competent to handle the matter. See Rule 1.1.

[8]   Paragraph (e) does not prohibit or regulate division of fees to be received in the future for work done when lawyers were previously associated in a law firm.

Disputes over Fees

[9]   If a procedure has been established for resolution of fee disputes, such as an arbitration or mediation procedure established by the bar, the lawyer must comply with the procedure when it is mandatory, and, even when it is voluntary, the lawyer should conscientiously consider submitting to it. Law may prescribe a procedure for determining a lawyer's fee, for example, in representation of an executor or administrator, a class or a person entitled to a reasonable fee as part of the measure of damages. The lawyer entitled to such a fee and a lawyer representing another party concerned with the fee should comply with the prescribed procedure.

Appendix G
California State Bar Rules

California State Bar Rule of Professional Conduct 4-200

Rule 4-200. Fees for Legal Services

(A) A member shall not enter into an agreement for, charge, or collect an illegal or unconscionable fee.

(B) Unconscionability of a fee shall be determined on the basis of all the facts and circumstances existing at the time the agreement is entered into except where the parties contemplate that the fee will be affected by later events. Among the factors to be considered, where appropriate, in determining the conscionability of a fee are the following:

(1) The amount of the fee in proportion to the value of the services performed.

(2) The relative sophistication of the member and the client.

(3) The novelty and difficulty of the questions involved and the skill requisite to perform the legal service properly.

(4) The likelihood, if apparent to the client, that the acceptance of the particular employment will preclude other employment by the member.

(5) The amount involved and the results obtained.

(6) The time limitations imposed by the client or by the circumstances.

(7) The nature and length of the professional relationship with the client.

(8) The experience, reputation, and ability of the member or members performing the services.

(9) Whether the fee is fixed or contingent.

(10) The time and labor required.

(11) The informed consent of the client to the fee.

California Business and Professions Code Section 6148

§ 6148. Written Fee Contract: Contents; Effect of Noncompliance

(a) In any case not coming within Section 6147 in which it is reasonably foreseeable that total expense to a client, including attorney fees, will exceed one thousand dollars ($1,000), the contract for services in the case shall be in writing. At the time the contract is entered into, the lawyer shall provide a duplicate copy of the contract signed by both the lawyer and the client, or the client's guardian or representative, to the client or to the client's guardian or representative. The written contract shall contain all of the following:

(1) Any basis of compensation including, but not limited to, hourly rates, statutory fees or flat fees, and other standard rates, fees, and charges applicable to the case.

(2) The general nature of the legal services to be provided to the client.

(3) The respective responsibilities of the lawyer and the client as to the performance of the contract.

(4) If the lawyer does not meet any of the following criteria, a statement disclosing that fact:

(A) Maintains errors and omissions insurance coverage.

(B) Has filed with the State Bar an executed copy of a written agreement guaranteeing payment of all claims established against the lawyer by his or her clients for errors or omissions arising out of the practice of law by the lawyer in the amount specified in paragraph (c) of subdivision (1) of Section B of Rule IV of the Law Corporation Rules of the State Bar. The State Bar may charge a filing fee not to exceed five dollars ($5).

(C) If a law corporation, has filed with the State Bar an executed copy of the written agreement required pursuant to paragraph (a), (b), or (c) of subsection (1) of Section B of Rule IV of the Law Corporation Rules of the State Bar.

(b)   All bills rendered by a lawyer to a client shall clearly state the basis thereof. Bills for the fee portion of the bill shall include the amount, rate, basis for calculation, or other method of determination of the lawyer's fees and costs. Bills for the cost and expense portion of the bill shall clearly identify the costs and expenses incurred and the amount of the costs and expenses. Upon request by the client, the lawyer shall provide a bill to the client no later than 10 days following the request unless the lawyer has provided a bill to the client within 31 days prior to the request, in which case the lawyer may provide a bill to the client no later than 31 days following the date the most recent bill was provided. The client is entitled to make similar requests at intervals of no less than 30 days following the initial request. In providing responses to client requests for billing information, the lawyer may use billing data that is currently effective on the date of the request, or, if any fees or costs to that date cannot be accurately determined, they shall be described and estimated.

(c)   Failure to comply with any provision of this section renders the agreement voidable at the option of the client, and the lawyer shall, upon the agreement being voided, be entitled to collect a reasonable fee.

(d)   This section shall not apply to any of the following:

(1) Services rendered in an emergency to avoid foreseeable prejudice to the rights or interests of the client or where a writing is otherwise impracticable.

(2) An arrangement as to the fee implied by the fact that the lawyer's services are of the same general kind as previously rendered to and paid for by the client.

(3) If the client knowingly states in writing, after full disclosure of this section, that a writing concerning fees is not required.

(4) If the client is a corporation.

(e)   This section applies prospectively only to fee agreements following its operative date.

(f)   This section shall remain in effect only until January 1, 2000, and as of that date is repealed, unless a later enacted statute, which is enacted before January 1, 2000, deletes or extends that date. (Added by Stats. 1986, ch. 475. Amended by Stats. 1990, ch. 483; Stats. 1992, ch. 1265; Stats. 1993, ch. 982; Stats. 1994, ch. 479; Stats. 1996, ch. 1104.)

California Business and Professions Code Section 6149

§ 6149. Written Fee Contract Confidential Communication

A written fee contract shall be deemed to be a confidential communication within the meaning of subdivision (e) of Section 6068 and of Section 952 of the Evidence Code. (Added by Stats. 1986, ch. 475.)

Appendix H
SAMPLE DETAILED BILL

Joseph J. Lawyer
123 Alphabet Lane
Anytown, NY 10014
202.555.1234

June 4, 2002
Trina Client
Client Incorporated
567 Numeral Parkway
Anytown, NY 10014

Matter: Real Estate Purchase

BILL FOR PROFESSIONAL SERVICES RENDERED

DATE	DESCRIPTION	LAWYER	TIME	RATE	TOTAL
10/01/02	Initial office conference and discussion with client concerning his primary goals and interests in selling industrial property located in downtown Atlanta. Client's stated primary goal is price rather than speed of sale.	Lawyer A	2.0	$220	$440
10/02/02	Telephone discussion with counsel for prospective buyer. Successfully increased the offering price for consideration by $100,000 in exchange for lowering mortgage interest rate from 10% to 8%.	Lawyer B	1.5	$180	$270

DATE	DESCRIPTION	LAWYER	TIME	RATE	TOTAL
10/02/02	Telephone conference with client to confirm his acceptance of modifications to transaction in addition to clarifying specifics and timing of future events preparatory to achieving a closing of the sale.	Lawyer A	.5	$220	$110
10/07/02	Conference at real estate office to establish criteria for closing satisfactory to both parties to the transaction	Lawyer B	2.5	$180	$ 450
10/10/02	Telephone conference with client to address final concerns to the expressed satisfaction of client in advance of closing.	Lawyer A	1.0	$220	$ 220
			SUBTOTAL		$1,490

EXPENSES:

DATE	DESCRIPTION		TOTAL
10/06/02	Postage		$ 13.00
10/02/02	Telephone call to opposing counsel		$ 19.25
		SUBTOTAL	$ 32.25

TOTAL DUE NOW — $ 1,522.25

Appendix I
TABS III

http://www.stilegal.com

Using TABS III to Manage Your Accounts Receivable

Managing accounts receivable is a critical part of any business. TABS III includes the tools necessary to effectively manage your accounts receivable.

Breaking Down Accounts Receivable

Billable items are classified as fees and costs. TABS III further classifies costs as expenses and advances with the additional ability to categorize costs by user-defined Cost Type. Up to 20 separate Cost Types can be defined—10 for expenses and 10 for costs. For example, you may want to classify travel expenses and courier expenses as their own separate categories.

TABS III lets you define up to five custom aging periods, which is useful for firms that need more flexibility than the standard 0–30, 31–60, 61–90, 91–120, and 121–180 aging periods.

Entering Billable Time and Costs

Billable items can be entered into TABS III using a variety of methods. In TABS III, each user can enter fees or costs using a detailed data entry screen or an abbreviated rapid data entry screen. STI's companion practice management software, PracticeMaster, offers true bidirectional synchronization. Fees and costs can be entered in either TABS III or PracticeMaster and are *automatically* synchronized with the other product.

TABS III allows data entry from many other sources. STI's Accounts Payable System (APS) will generate cost transactions in TABS III when an invoice or check transaction is entered. Payment transactions can be automatically generated from STI's Trust Accounting System to transfer funds to a client's account to pay the client's balance for fees and costs. TABS III Remote allows data entry from remote terminals or a laptop. STI has off-the-shelf interface programs for over 40 different collection devices for cost recovery such as photocopies, fax, and postage machines. A conversion programming staff provides customized solutions giving you the potential ability to import any data from any source. Additionally, interface programs are available allowing you to import information from Timeslips®, Time Matters®, Amicus®, and other popular software programs. A standard interface program can be used to import fees and costs from any source that can provide the data in STI's specified data file format.

	Billable Items		
Means of Capturing Billable Items	**Time/ Fees**	**Client Costs/ Checks**	**Trust Funds**
TABS III	X	X	X
TABS III Remote	X	X	
Palm OS® Handheld	X	X	
STI's Accounts Payable System		X	
STI's Trust Accounting System			X
Collection Devices		X	
PracticeMaster	X	X	
Other (i.e., Time Matters, Timeslips, Amicus, etc.)	X	X	X

Trust Funds and Client Funds

For trust funds and client retainers, TABS III includes a built-in Client Funds feature that handles separate accounting for retainer and escrow accounts. You can bill a one-time retainer until it has been paid as well as replenish a pre-established minimum balance. For advanced funds handling with check reconciliation, STI's Trust Accounting System (TAS) handles unlimited trust accounts that are maintained in up to nine separate bank accounts. Client Funds balances or TAS balances are included on statements, Accounts receivable reports, and other reports, and are easily accessible in TABS III's Client Manager and Client windows.

Receipts

Payments are entered using TABS III's payment program. A single payment can be entered for one client or easily applied to multiple clients for situations where you have multiple matters for a single client. The Payment data entry program shows the client's accounts receivable right on the data entry screen. Payments can be specifically applied to fees, expenses, or advances. You have the ability to apply the payment to a client's aggregate balance or to a specific invoice.

A Cash Receipts Report shows all payments for clients for a specified data range. Once payments have been processed, they will appear on a Processed Payments Report thus providing an audit trail of how each processed payment was allocated. This report shows exactly how individual payments were allocated to fees, expenses, advances, sales tax, and finance charge. A detail option lets you see the exact allocation to individual timekeepers and Cost Types.

When integrating with QuickBooks® from Intuit or STI's General Ledger System (GLS), you can specify which accounts the payment will be applied to in your general ledger accounting software.

How Accounts Receivable Is Created

Billing clients creates accounts receivable. TABS III provides specialized handling of the various types of billing used by law firms, including:

- Contingency Billing
- Retainer Billing
- Flat Fee Billing and Value Billing
- Task Code Billing (ABA Uniform Task-Based Management System)
- Hourly Billing
- Progressive Billing with Reconciliation
- Split Fee Billing
- Threshold Billing
- Electronic Billing (requires "Taskbill" module)

Accounts receivable is created in TABS III after items have been billed on a final statement and updated. Statements can be run individually or in batches. TABS III's Pre-Bill Tracking feature makes it a snap for administrative staff to track the status of draft and final statements. For example, you can run separate batches of draft statements for each lawyer. As draft statements are approved, they can be tagged as "Reviewed," thus making it very simple to run a batch of final statements for all approved statements.

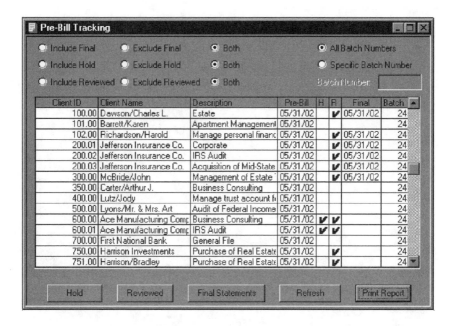

Viewing and Analyzing Accounts Receivable

Accounts receivable can be quickly viewed via the Client Manager. After selecting the client, the total amount due is automatically shown. Click the **AR Balance** button and a detailed aged breakdown is shown along with trust account balances. Multiple report icons can be customized on the Client Manager window, and Client Manager AR window making is as easy as clicking a button to view the desired reports.

Once statements have been updated, Accounts receivable reports can be run for individual clients, a range or "pick list" of clients, or all clients. TABS III offers a great deal of flexibility in how reports can be run. Similar to TABS III's other reports, the accounts receivable reports can be run for:

- ◆ the entire firm
- ◆ by originating, primary, or secondary timekeeper
- ◆ by area of productivity
- ◆ by location
- ◆ by client
- ◆ by billing frequency
- ◆ by aging period

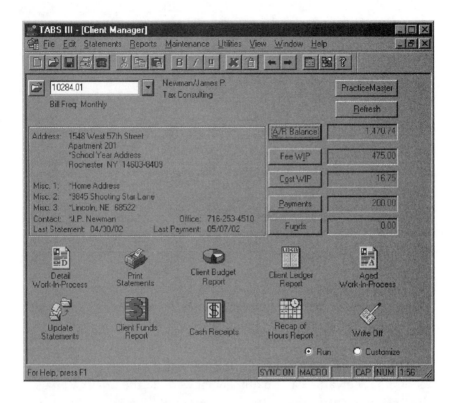

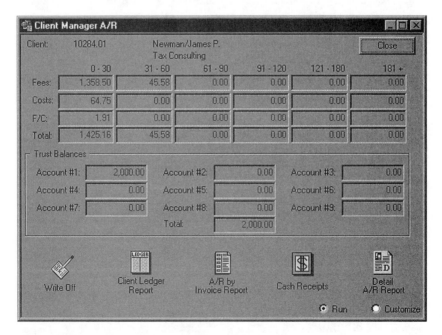

The **Summary Accounts-Receivable Report** is a compact snapshot and shows one line for each client with receivables broken down by aging period.

Date: 02/15/02			TABS III Summary Accounts Receivable Report				Page: 1
			Burns, Jensen & Powers, P.C.				

Primary Timekeeper: 1 Robert J. Burns

Client Name	0-30	31-60	61-90	91-120	121-180	181+	Bal Due
910.00M Richardson/Jim	0.00	0.00	0.00	1195.00	0.00	0.00	1195.00
920.00M Carter/Sally	0.00	175.00	0.00	0.00	850.00	0.00	1025.00
940.00M Kiltzer/George	0.00	225.00	0.00	1535.00	0.00	0.00	1760.00
Totals	0.00	400.00	0.00	2730.00	850.00	0.00	3980.00

The **Detail Accounts-Receivable Report** shows aged receivables for fees, expenses, advances, and finance charge. Additional information such as the last statement date, last payment date and amount, and unbilled work-in-process is also shown.

Various options are available when running the accounts receivable reports that make it easy to identify problematic clients. For example, a "Select Age of Past Due Clients to Print" option lets you easily include only those clients with past due amounts over a specified number of days. The "Only Print Clients with No Payments in the last ___ Days" option lets you quickly identify those clients who have not made a payment in a certain amount of time. A "Minimum

```
Date: 02/15/02    TABS III Detail Accounts Receivable Report    Page: 1
                     Burns, Jensen & Powers, P.C.

Primary Timekeeper: 1 Robert J. Burns

                        Age      Fees    Expenses  Advances   Fin Chg      Total

       910.00M Richardson/Jim
            RE: Settlement of Estate

Open Date: 10/17/01    0-30:     0.00      0.00      0.00      0.00        0.00
Last Bill: 11/01/01   31-60:     0.00      0.00      0.00      0.00        0.00
Last Pymt: mm/dd/yy   61-90:     0.00      0.00      0.00      0.00        0.00
                     91-120:  1150.00     45.00      0.00      0.00     1195.00
                    121-180:     0.00      0.00      0.00      0.00        0.00
                       181+:     0.00      0.00      0.00      0.00        0.00
                    Balance:  1150.00     45.00      0.00      0.00     1195.00
(WIP)Fees:     0.00 Exps:        0.00   Advs:        0.00   Total:        0.00
     Age: 0
```

Balance" option lets you filter out clients whose balance is under a specified threshold. As an example, combining these options lets you generate a report for all clients who have a balance greater than $500 that is over 90 days past due and who have not made a payment in 30 days.

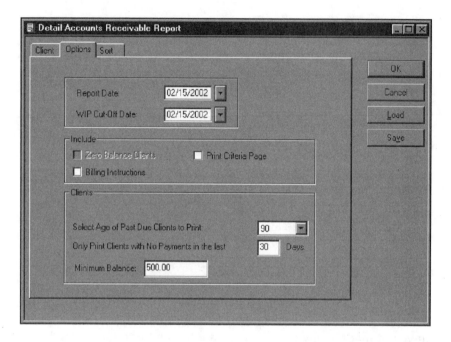

An **Accounts Receivable by Invoice Report** can be run that breaks down billed and due amounts of individual statements by fees, expenses, advances, tax, and finance charge. You can optionally break down fees by individual lawyer and expenses and advances by individual cost type.

A **Client Ledger Report** replaces your manual client ledger cards for past billing and payment information. Individual statement detail is shown with a running balance.

A **Client Billing Summary Report** additionally breaks down individual statements by fees, expenses, advances, fee sales tax, expense sales tax, advance sales tax, and finance charge.

TABS III lets you customize and save report defaults using their Report Definitions. A Report Suites feature lets you group selected

Report Definitions and run them as a batch. These features make it easy to run the same batch of reports on a regular basis.

Collections

The Client Notes feature lets you track ad hoc notes regarding the client including billing arrangements and collections information. Designate these notes as "Billing Instructions" and you will be given the option to include them on the accounts receivable reports, WIP reports, and draft statements.

A special "Reminder Statements" check box in the Statements program automates the process of running reminder statements.

Modifying or Undoing Accounts Receivable

In a perfect world, accounts receivable do not need to be changed. However, there always seem to be situations that occur that require unique handling. TABS III provides various methods of undoing accounts receivable. Credit transactions can be entered and processed. Payments can be adjusted by being reversed or refunded. Accounts receivable balances can be transferred from one client to another client. Accounts receivable balances can be written off partially or in their entirety. You can configure TABS III to allow or disallow editing of accounts receivable balances. TABS III provides the ability to completely reverse an entire statement even after it has been updated. Previously updated statements can be reprinted at any time. Like all functions in TABS III, you choose which users will be granted access rights to these functions.

Summary

TABS III offers a lot of power and flexibility for the price. It is scalable and allows your firm to grow without outgrowing the software. The vendor, Software Technology, Inc., has been providing quality software for law firms since 1979.

PCLAW

http://www.pclaw.com

Creating, Tracking, and Collecting AR Using Technology (PCLaw)

The ability to track and manage AR is critical to the business of a law firm.

Technology gives a law firm an advantage over firms that use a manual system to manage their AR effectively.

AR occurs through a series of steps including:

1) Capturing billable items (time, fees, costs, and trust funds).
2) Creating AR (Billing)
3) Managing AR (Using data effectively to make management decisions and to help in the collection of AR).

1. Capturing Billable Items

AR in a law office is made up of billed items including time, fees, trust funds, and client costs. To effectively manage AR law firms must first ensure that these components can be easily entered into their system by all of the firm's staff.

Capturing Billable Time Matrix

Billable Items			
Means of Capturing Billable Items	**Time/ Fees**	**Client Costs/ Checks**	**Trust Funds**
Desktop PC	X	X	X
Web Browser	X	X*	
Palm OS Device	X	X*	
Non-networked PC	X	X*	
Case Management System (Amicus Attorney and Time Matters)	X		
Cost Recovery Devices		X*	

*Client costs can be captured but checks can be created only from the desktop PC

Tracking Time and Fees

Time and fees can be captured in variety of ways, making it easy for all firms' staff members to capture more billable time. Staff working in the office can capture time and fees using a traditional time sheet or use a pop-up timer when a billable event occurs. Additionally, appointments in PCLaw's Calendar can automatically be converted into time entries once they are completed.

Firms using Case Management Systems (Time Matters and Amicus Attorney) can use these programs to send time and fees across to PCLaw ready for billing.

Staff working away from the office can use a Web Browser (ePCLaw), their Palm OS Device (PCLaw TE), and a non-networked computer (Satellite Remote Module).

Capturing Client Costs

Law firms can capture client costs for checks written on behalf of clients and for noncash disbursements (for example, in-house photocopies). PCLaw is integrated, so writing a check on behalf of a client gets charged on the client ledger and on the bank journal in one easy step. PCLaw can also import client costs from third-party cost recovery devices (for example, fax machines).

2. Creating AR (Billing)

The creation of AR is often a long, tedious process for a law firm because of the special requirements that legal billing commands. The simpler the billing process can be made, the quicker bills can be sent out and payments collected.

Legal-Specific Billing Issues

PCLaw will handle the following billing arrangements:

- ◆ ABA Task-Based Billing
- ◆ Split Billing
- ◆ Contingency Billing
- ◆ Flat-Fee and Hourly Billing
- ◆ Electronic Billing (requires optional module)

Easy Billing

PCLaw includes client billing controls that make it easy to bill matters individually or en mass. Law firm invoices normally go through a series of changes and approvals by the lawyers before they are sent to clients. PCLaw provides a prebilling function with bill formats that make it easy for lawyers to make changes to the bills before they are sent out. (Show format) Additionally bills can easily be changed before and after billing.

Customizable Bill Formats

PCLaw comes complete with a range of common bill formats. Users can create their own formats or modify existing ones to suit their needs. Each client can have their own separate format so a firm can meet the individual needs of their clients. Bills can include time fees, trust activity, payments, retainer replenishment requests, and past activity.

3. Managing and Collecting AR

Once the AR has been effectively entered into PCLaw, a law firm can then use reports and functions to help manage and collect AR.
   Having accurate AR data in PCLaw:

- ◆ Makes it easier to manage the firm by providing tools to assess the AR from different angles.
- ◆ Provides staff members with quick access to AR details allowing the firm to better serve their clients.
- ◆ Aids staff in the process of collecting payments.

AR Reporting for Everyone in the Firm

PCLaw includes a host of AR reports that can be used to assess AR from different angles including:

- ◆ Responsible lawyer
- ◆ Fee credit lawyer—Helps the firm assess lawyer productivity and compensation
- ◆ Type of law—Summarizing AR reports by type of law provides you with productivity figures by area of practice

- ◆ Client—Client-detailed AR balances along with payment information let you assess your most profitable clients.
- ◆ Aging—Running AR reports by aging categories helps you determine clients with oldest balances. This helps the firm to determine which clients may need a reminder about their past balances or their accounts may need to be written off.

Write Up/Down Reports

PCLaw makes it easy to write up/down invoices. Write up/down reports let you keep track of changes to invoices highlighting potential problem clients.

Payment and Collection Reports

PCLaw's ability to handle fee splits between partners on a per-file basis makes it easy to manage payments and improves the firm's ability to compensate lawyers based on collections. The Payment Allocation Listing breaks up payments between fees, costs, and taxes.

Simplify Collection of AR

One of the most useful tools in PCLaw is the Receivables By Client report. This report shows details on amounts billed but not fully paid for each client. The report includes the client's name, address, phone, and fax for quick follow-up. Additionally, notes can be recorded on the client files when attempting to collect payments. These "collection notes" can then be printed on the OCR report, making it easy for any staff member to have the history on hand when attempting to collect payment. You can age the Receivables By Client report to highlight delinquent clients, and Trust funds are also displayed for each client so you know which matters are eligible for trust transfers to pay off their balances.

Past-Due-Notices Module

The Past Due Notices can be printed at any time for clients with overdue accounts, to stimulate payment, and minimize bad debt write-off. Interest can be applied to overdue balances, and phrases can be customized to reflect the aging of the balance.

On-Screen Functions

The Quick Client Summary function gives the user instant access to AR information for any client. Clicking on the AR balance brings up invoice details that make up the AR balance. This tool is useful for any staff member who wants a quick means of finding out AR information and details without having to run a report.

Case Management (Time Matters and Amicus Attorney)

Time Matters and Amicus Attorney case management systems both have the ability to display client AR balances from PCLaw.

Appendix J
COLLECTION SCHEDULE

COLLECTION PROCEDURES BY DAY—SAMPLE SCHEDULE

Day	Action	Description
0–30		Prepare and record time entries hourly/daily as work proceeds.
27		Prepare pre-bills for review.
30		Submit corrections to pre-bills and any additions for days 27–30.
33		Mail billing statements/invoices.
78	Phone call #1	Collection Manager calls to remind client.
83	Collection #1	Letter signed by Collection Manager is sent to overdue accounts.
93	Phone call #2	Collection Manager calls to see if there is a problem with bill.
108	Collection #2	Letter signed by Collection Manager is sent to overdue accounts.
123	Phone call #3	Collection Manager calls to insist that payment be made.
138	Collection #3	Letter signed by Collection Manager is sent to overdue accounts.
153	Phone call #4	Collection Manager calls to ask for payment before account is turned over to Collection Agency.
183	Collection #4	Letter, which is signed by Collection Manager and gives due date before account is sent to collections, is sent to overdue accounts.
213	Collection Agency	Account is sent to Collection Agency by Collections Manager.

Appendix K
COLLECTION LETTER #1

Date:

Joseph Client
1234 Alphabet Way
Anytown, New York 20034

Dear Mr. Client:

Our records indicate that your account with us is now past due. We would greatly appreciate your bringing your account current within the next seven (7) days.

Your current outstanding balance is $ _____.

Please call me if you have any questions about your account. Otherwise, we look forward to receiving payment within the week.

Thank you for your understanding and cooperation in this matter.

Sincerely,

Jane Addams
Collections Supervisor

cc: billing partner

COLLECTION LETTER #2

Date:

Joseph Client
1234 Alphabet Way
Anytown, New York 20034

Dear Mr. Client:

I have reviewed your outstanding account; your account has a balance due of $ _____ which is now more than ____ days past due.

Our previous correspondence to you has not been answered. If you have questions or concerns about your account, please call me so that we can resolve any difficulties. Otherwise, I will look forward to receiving payment by _____ (date).

Thank you.

Sincerely,

Jane Addams
Collections Supervisor

cc: billing partner

COLLECTION LETTER #3

Date:

Joseph Client
1234 Alphabet Way
Anytown, New York 20034

Dear Mr. Client:

Your account with our firm is now long past due. I have tried on previous occasions to communicate with you about this account, but to no avail. Since the firm has not received payment from you, we will now review our options and consider turning your account over to a collection agency.

We value our business relationship with you and would like to resolve this issue as quickly as possible without the intervention of third parties.

Please send a check to us for the total amount of $_____ by _____ (date).

Thank you.

Sincerely,

Jane Addams
Collections Supervisor

cc: billing partner

COLLECTION LETTER #4

Date:

Joseph Client
1234 Alphabet Way
Anytown, New York 20034

Dear Mr. Client:

Your account is delinquent. I have sent you letters and called you to discuss the situation, but you have not responded.

Because you have not contacted us, the firm has no choice but to turn your account over to a collection agency.

To avoid dealing with (name of collection agency), send us a check for the outstanding balance of $_____ before _____ .

If we do not receive your check by _____ (date), we will turn your account over for collection.

Thank you.

Sincerely,

Jane Addams
Collections Supervisor

cc: billing partner

Appendix L
PROMISE TO PAY LETTER

Date:

Joseph Client
1234 Alphabet Way
Anytown, New York 20034

Dear Mr. Client:

In accord with our telephone conversation on _____ (date), you
agreed to pay the firm $_____ by _____ (date).

Thank you in advance for your consideration in this matter.

Thank you.

Sincerely,

Jane Addams
Collections Supervisor

cc: billing partner

PAYMENT RECEIVED LETTER

Date:

Joseph Client
1234 Alphabet Way
Anytown, New York 20034

Dear Mr. Client:

Thank you for your check in the amount of $____, which we received on ____ (date). Your remaining balance is now $____. Thank you for your cooperation in this matter.

Sincerely,

Jane Addams
Collections Supervisor

cc: billing partner

MISSED PAYMENT LETTER

Date:

Joseph Client
1234 Alphabet Way
Anytown, New York 20034

Dear Mr. Client:

I did not receive your scheduled payment of $ _____ as promised for _____ (date).

Please send the firm a check for this amount in accord with our accepted payment schedule. If there is a problem with this schedule, please notify us immediately; your failure to respond will necessitate further action for collection.

Thank you.

Sincerely,

Jane Addams
Collections Supervisor

cc: billing partner

Appendix M
AGING ANALYSIS REPORT—SAMPLE

Month of:

Name of Client	0–30 days	31–60 days	61–90 days	91–120 days	121–150 days	More than 150 days	TOTAL
Jones Inc.	$5,000	$3,000	$3,000				$11,000
ABC Corp.			$5,000	$500			5, 500
C Industries	$7,500	$5,000					12,500
Boston Products						$3,000	3,000
TOTAL	$12,500	$8,000	$8,000	$ 500	0	$3,000	$32,000

AGING ANALYSIS REPORT—BLANK

Month of:

Name of Client	0–30 days	31–60 days	61–90 days	91–120 days	121–150 days	More than 150 days	TOTAL
TOTAL							

Appendix N
ACCOUNTS RECEIVABLE AGING SCHEDULE BY PERCENTAGE BY QUARTER—SAMPLE

Days Outstanding	1st Quarter (Jan.–Mar.)	2nd Quarter (Apr.–Jun.)	3rd Quarter (Jul.–Sept.)	4th Quarter (Oct.–Dec.)
0–30 days	40%	45%	50%	53%
31–60 days	34%	20	18	14
61–90 days	15%	18	20	24
91–120 days	6%	5	4	4
121–150 days	3%	8	3	-0-
151+ days	2%	4	5	5
TOTAL	100%	100%	100%	100%

ACCOUNTS RECEIVABLE AGING SCHEDULE BY PERCENTAGE BY QUARTER—BLANK

Days Outstanding	1st Quarter (Jan.–Mar.)	2nd Quarter (Apr.–Jun.)	3rd Quarter (Jul.–Sept.)	4th Quarter (Oct.–Dec.)
0–30 days				
31–60 days				
61–90 days				
91–120 days				
121–150 days				
151+ days				
TOTAL				

Appendix O
OVERDUE ACCOUNT CALL SHEET

OVERDUE ACCOUNT CALL SHEET

Date: _____   ( ) I called   ( ) Client called

Time: _____Outstanding balance: _____Days past due: ____

Name of Person talked to: _____Position: _____

Name of Company: _____Telephone #: _____

File #:_____Billing Lawyer: _____

Previous Interaction:

_____

_____

_____

_____

My statements:	Client's statements:

Appendix P
SCRIPT FOR DIAL AND SMILE

"Hello, Mr./Ms. Client, this is Sally Collector from the law firm of XYZ. I'm calling about our bill. Did you receive our statement?"

- ◆ If the client says s/he did NOT receive the statement, the caller should immediately fax, messenger, or mail a copy of the statement to the client.

If the client has received the bill, the caller continues.

"Mr./Ms. Client, did you understand the statement?"

- ◆ If the answer is NO, the caller should tell the client that the billing lawyer will call shortly to answer any questions the client may have. Your clerk should now alert you that the client does not understand the bill. Call the client as soon as possible to clarify any misunderstandings the client may have.

If the client does understand the statement, the caller continues.

"Mr./Ms. Client, is there any problem with the bill?"

- ◆ If the answer is YES, the caller should ask for more information about the nature of the problem. The caller should then contact the lawyer immediately. The lawyer should call the client right away and deal with the issue appropriately under the circumstances.

If the client says, "No, there is no problem with the bill," the caller continues.

"Mr./Ms. Client, when can we expect to receive payment for that statement in our office?"

(not "When will the check be mailed?")

Normally, the client will make a commitment for a payment—often only a partial one. The clerk should mark the calendar for that date. Have the clerk attempt to get a commitment of no further than 10 days out.

If the check does not arrive on time, have the clerk call the client on the very next day and go through the same set of questions. Each set of calls should be approximately 10 days apart. Complete this process several times over a period of not more than six to eight weeks.

Index

Experian, 15
Extending credit, 9–10

Failure to collect, 67–70
 collection agencies, 68–69
 cutting your losses, 67–68
 filing suit, 69–70
 firm efforts, 68
 winning, 70
Fee agreement, 17–19, 88–93
Fees
 discounting, 64–65
 justification of, 41
File reviews, 70
File-opening checklist, 87
Filing suit, 36, 69–70
 file reviews, 70
 insurance company, 69
 pricing and, 36
 required activities, 69
 statute of limitations, 69
Financial ratios, 84
Firing the client, 36

Grisham, John, 13

Hardware, 50
Huxley, Julian, 7

Inability to pay, 63–64
Insurance company, 69
Intake interview, 8–9
Intake process, 7–16
 credit application, 11–13
 credit policy, 14–16
 extending credit, 9–10
 intake interview, 8–9
 lawyer as sleuth, 13–14
 new client intake forms, 77–83
Interest, 13, 15–16
Investigation, 13–14

Johnson, Samuel, 67

Lawyers
 compliance policy for, 58
 pricing responsibilities, 34
 as sleuth, 13–14

Legal service as commodity, 30–31
Letters
 calls and letters in tandem,
  57–58, 63
 collection letter, 57, 125–128
 engagement letter, 19–20
 missed payment letter, 131
 nonengagement letter, 86
 payment received letter, 130
 promise to pay letter, 129
Lincoln, Abraham, 33
Lines of credit, 15
Litigation budget sample, 99–100

Management tool, billing as, 40–41
Marketing opportunities, 45–46
Marx, Groucho, 39
Maugham, W. Somerset, 27
Merchant account, 72
Missed payment letter, 131
Model Rules, 101–108
Monthly billing, 42
Monthly reports, 58

N/C (no charge), 41
Needs analysis, 48–49
New client intake forms, 77–83
Nonengagement letter, 86

Original documents, 20
Overbilling, 64–65
Overdue account call sheet, 134
Overdue account form, 58

Parker, Dorothy, 1, 71
Payment concerns, 31–32
Payment received letter, 130
PCLaw, 48, 119–123
Periodic billing, 42–43
 monthly billing, 42
 more frequent billing, 42–43
 positive-result billing, 43
Phone calls, 57–58, 60–61, 63, 134
Policies
 collections policy, 55–58
 compliance policy, 58
 credit policy, 14–16, 56

About the CD

The accompanying CD contains the text of each of the Appendices (excluding Appendices F, G, and I) from *Collecting Your Fee: Getting Paid from Intake to Invoice*. The files are in Microsoft® Word 97 format.

For additional information about the files on the CD, please open and read the "readme.doc" file on the CD.

NOTE: The set of files on the CD may only be used on a single computer or moved to and used on another computer. Under no circumstances may the set of files be used on more than one computer at one time. If you are interested in obtaining a license to use the set of files on a local network, please contact: Director, Copyrights and Contracts, American Bar Association, 750 N. Lake Shore Drive, Chicago, IL 60611, (312) 988-6101. **Please read the license and warranty statements on the following page before using this CD.**

ABA
Defending Liberty
Pursuing Justice

CD-ROM to accompany
Collecting Your Fee: Getting Paid from Intake to Invoice

WARNING: Opening this package indicates your understanding and acceptance of the following Terms and Conditions.

READ THE FOLLOWING TERMS AND CONDITIONS BEFORE OPENING THIS SEALED PACKAGE. IF YOU DO NOT AGREE WITH THEM, PROMPTLY RETURN THE UNOPENED PACKAGE TO EITHER THE PARTY FROM WHOM IT WAS ACQUIRED OR TO THE AMERICAN BAR ASSOCIATION AND YOUR MONEY WILL BE RETURNED.

The document files in this package are a proprietary product of the American Bar Association and are protected by Copyright Law. The American Bar Association retains title to and ownership of these files.

License

You may use this set of files on a single computer or move it to and use it on another computer, but under no circumstances may you use the set of files on more than one computer at the same time. You may copy the files either in support of your use of the files on a single computer or for backup purposes. If you are interested in obtaining a license to use the set of files on a local network, please contact: Manager, Publication Policies & Contracting, American Bar Association, 750 N. Lake Shore Drive, Chicago, IL 60611, (312) 988-6101.

You may permanently transfer the set of files to another party if the other party agrees to accept the terms and conditions of this License Agreement. If you transfer the set of files, you must at the same time transfer all copies of the files to the same party or destroy those not transferred. Such transfer terminates your license. You may not rent, lease, assign or otherwise transfer the files except as stated in this paragraph.

You may modify these files for your own use within the provisions of this License Agreement. You may not redistribute any modified files.

Warranty

If a CD-ROM in this package is defective, the American Bar Association will replace it at no charge if the defective diskette is returned to the American Bar Association within 60 days from the date of acquisition.

American Bar Association warrants that these files will perform in substantial compliance with the documentation supplied in this package. However, the American Bar Association does not warrant these forms as to the correctness of the legal material contained therein. If you report a significant defect in performance in writing to the American Bar Association, and the American Bar Association is not able to correct it within 60 days, you may return the diskettes, including all copies and documentation, to the American Bar Association and the American Bar Association will refund your money.

Any files that you modify will no longer be covered under this warranty even if they were modified in accordance with the License Agreement and product documentation.

IN NO EVENT WILL THE AMERICAN BAR ASSOCIATION, ITS OFFICERS, MEMBERS, OR EMPLOYEES BE LIABLE TO YOU FOR ANY DAMAGES, INCLUDING LOST PROFITS, LOST SAVINGS OR OTHER INCIDENTAL OR CONSEQUENTIAL DAMAGES ARISING OUT OF YOUR USE OR INABILITY TO USE THESE FILES EVEN IF THE AMERICAN BAR ASSOCIATION OR AN AUTHORIZED AMERICAN BAR ASSOCIATION REPRESENTATIVE HAS BEEN ADVISED OF THE POSSIBILITY OF SUCH DAMAGES, OR FOR ANY CLAIM BY ANY OTHER PARTY. SOME STATES DO NOT ALLOW THE LIMITATION OR EXCLUSION OF LIABILITY FOR INCIDENTAL OR CONSEQUENTIAL DAMAGES, IN WHICH CASE THIS LIMITATION MAY NOT APPLY TO YOU.

Order Form

Qty	Title	LPM Price	Reg Price	Total
_____	ABA Guide to Lawyer Trust Accounts (5110374)	69.95	79.95	$_____
_____	Changing Jobs, 3rd Ed. (511-0425)	39.95	49.95	$_____
_____	Compensation Plans for Lawyers, 3rd Ed. (5110452)	74.95	89.95	$_____
_____	Complete Guide to Marketing Your Law Practice (5110428)	74.95	89.95	$_____
_____	Complete Internet Handbook for Lawyers (5110413)	39.95	49.95	$_____
_____	Do-It-Yourself Public Relations (5110352)	69.95	79.95	$_____
_____	Easy Self-Audits for the Busy Law Firm (511-0420P)	99.95	84.95	$_____
_____	Essential Formbook, Vols. I and II	*Please call for information*		
_____	Flying Solo, Third Edition (511-0463)	79.95	89.95	$_____
_____	Handling Personnel Issues in the Law Office (5110381)	59.95	69.95	$_____
_____	HotDocs in One Hour for Lawyers, Second Edition (5110464)	29.95	34.95	$_____
_____	How to Build & Manage an Employment Law Practice (5110389)	44.95	54.95	$_____
_____	How to Build & Manage a Personal Injury Practice (5110386)	44.95	54.95	$_____
_____	How to Start & Build a Law Practice, Fourth Edition (5110415)	57.95	69.95	$_____
_____	Law Firm Partnership Guide: Strengthening Your Firm (5110391)	64.95	74.95	$_____
_____	Law Firm Partnership Guide: Getting Started (5110363)	64.95	74.95	$_____
_____	Law Office Policy & Procedures Manual, 4th Ed. (5110441)	109.95	129.95	$_____
_____	Law Office Staff Manual for Solos & Small Firms, 2nd Ed. (5110445)	59.95	69.95	$_____
_____	Lawyer's Guide to Marketing on the Internet, 2nd Ed. (5110484)	69.95	79.95	$_____
_____	Legal Career Guide, 4th Ed. (5110479)	29.95	34.95	$_____
_____	Living with the Law (5110379)	59.95	69.95	$_____
_____	Making Partner, Second Edition (511-0482)	39.95	49.95	$_____
_____	Managing Partner 101, Second Edition (5110451)	44.95	49.95	$_____
_____	Persuasive Computer Presentations (511-0462)	69.95	79.95	$_____
_____	Practicing Law Without Clients (5110376)	49.95	59.95	$_____
_____	Running a Law Practice on a Shoestring (5110387)	39.95	49.95	$_____
_____	Successful Client Newsletters (5110396)	39.95	44.95	$_____
_____	Telecommuting for Lawyers (5110401)	39.95	49.95	$_____
_____	Through the Client's Eyes, 2nd Ed. (5110480)	69.95	79.95	$_____
_____	Wills, Trusts, and Technology (5430377)	74.95	84.95	$_____
_____	Winning Alternatives to the Billable Hour, 2nd Ed. (5110483)	129.95	149.95	$_____

*Handling
$10.00-$24.99 . . . . $3.95
$25.00-$49.99 . . . . $4.95
$50.00+ $5.95

**Tax
DC residents add 5.75%
IL residents add 8.75%
MD residents add 5%

Subtotal	$_____
*Handling	$_____
**Tax	$_____
TOTAL	$_____

PAYMENT
❏ **Check enclosed (to the ABA)**   ❏ **Bill Me**
❏ Visa   ❏ MasterCard   ❏ American Express

_____
Account Number   Exp. Date   Signature

Name _____ Firm _____
Address _____
City _____ State _____ Zip _____
Phone Number _____ E-mail address _____

Mail: ABA Publication Orders, P.O. Box 10892, Chicago, Illinois 60610-0892
◆ **Phone: (800) 285-2221** ◆ **FAX: (312) 988-5568**
E-Mail: abasvcctr@abanet.org ◆ **Internet: http://www.abanet.org/lpm/catalog**

Source Code: 22AEND499

THE ABA LAW PRACTICE MANAGEMENT SECTION

The ABA Guide to Lawyer Trust Accounts. Details ways that lawyers should manage trust accounts to comply with ethical & statutory requirements.

Changing Jobs, 3rd Edition. A handbook designed to help lawyers make changes in their professional careers. Includes career planning advice from dozens of experts.

Compensation Plans for Law Firms, 3rd Ed. This third edition discusses the basics for a fair and simple compensation system for partners, of counsel, associates, paralegals, and staff.

Complete Guide to Marketing Your Law Practice. Filled with dozens of fresh and innovative ideas, this book features the strategies form the country's top legal marketers.

Complete Internet Handbook for Lawyers. A thorough orientation to the Internet, including e-mail, search engines, conducting research and marketing on the Internet, publicizing a Web site, Net ethics, security, viruses, and more. Features a updated, companion Web site with forms you can download and customize.

Do-It-Yourself Public Relations. A hands-on guide (and diskette!) for lawyers with public relations ideas, sample letters, and forms.

Easy Self-Audits for the Busy Law Office. Dozens of evaluation tools help you determine what's working (and what's not) in your law office or legal department. You'll discover several opportunities for improving productivity and efficiency along the way!

Essential Formbook: Comprehensive Management Tools for Lawyers, Vols. I & II. Useful to legal practitioners of all specialties and sizes, the first two volumes of *The Essential Formbook* include more than 100 forms, checklists, and sample documents. And, with all the forms on disk, it's easy to modify them to match your specific needs.

Flying Solo: A Survival Guide for the Solo Lawyer, Third Edition. This book gives solos, as well as small firms, all the information needed to build a successful practice. Contains 55 chapters covering office location, billing and cash flow, computers and equipment, and much more.

Handling Personnel Issues in the Law Office. Packed with tips on "safely" and legally recruiting, hiring, training, managing, and terminating employees.

HotDocs in One Hour for Lawyers, Second Edition. Offers simple instructions, ranging from generating a document from a template to inserting conditional text and creating dialogs.

How to Build and Manage an Employment Law Practice. Provides clear guidance and valuable tips for solo or small employment law practices, including preparation, marketing, accepting cases, and managing workload and finances. Includes several time-saving "fill in the blank" forms.

How to Build and Manage a Personal Injury Practice. Features all of the tactics, technology, and tools needed for a profitable practice, including how to: write a sound business plan, develop a financial forecast, choose office space, market your practice, and more.

How to Start and Build a Law Practice, 4th Edition. Jay Foonberg's classic guide has been completely updated and expanded! Features 128 chapters, including 30 new ones, that reveal secrets to successful planning, marketing, billing, client relations, and much more. Chock-full of forms, sample letters, and checklists, including a sample business plan, "The Foonberg Law Office Management Checklist," and more.

Law Firm Partnership Guide: Strengthening Your Firm. Addresses what to do after your firm is up and running, including how to handle: change, financial problems, governance issues, compensating firm owners, and leadership.

Law Firm Partnership Guide: Getting Started. Examines the most important issues you must consider to ensure your partnership's success, including self-assessment, organization structure, written agreements, financing, and basic operations. Includes *A Model Partnership Agreement* on diskette.

Law Office Policy and Procedures Manual, 4th Ed. A model for law office policies and procedures (includes diskette). Covers law office organization, management, personnel policies, financial management, technology, and communications systems.

Law Office Staff Manual for Solos and Small Firms, Second Editon. Use this manual as is or customize it using the book's diskette. Includes general office policies on confidentiality, employee compensation, sick leave, sexual harassment, billing, and more.

The Lawyer's Guide to Marketing on the Internet, Second Edition. This book provides you with countless Internet marketing possibilities and shows you how to effectively and effieciently market your law practice on the Internet.

Legal Career Guide: From Law Student to Lawyer, Fourth Edition is a step-by-step guide for planning a law career, preparing and executing a job search, and moving into the market. This book is perfect for students currently choosing a career path, or simply deciding if law school is right for them.

Living with the Law: Strategies to Avoid Burnout and Create Balance. Examines ways to manage stress, make the practice of law more satisfying, and improve client service.

Making Partner: A Guide for Law Firm Associates, Second Edition. If you are serious about making partner, this book will help you formulate your step-by-step plan and be your guide for years to come for your decisions and actions within your firm.

Managing Partner 101: A Guide to Successful Law Firm Leadership is designed to help managing partners, lawyers, and other legal professionals understand the role and responsibilities of a law firm's managing partner.

Persuasive Computer Presentations: The Essential Guide for Lawyers explains the advantages of computer presentation resources, how to use them, what they can do, and the legal issues involved in their use. It covers how to use computer presentations in the courtroom and during meetings, pretrial, and seminars.

Practicing Law Without Clients: Making a Living as a Freelance Lawyer. Describes freelance legal researching, writing, and consulting opportunities that are available to lawyers.

Running a Law Practice on a Shoestring. Offers a crash course in successful entrepreneurship. Features money-saving tips on office space, computer equipment, travel, furniture, staffing, and more.

Successful Client Newsletters. Written for lawyers, editors, writers, and marketers, this book can help you to start a newsletter from scratch, redesign an existing one, or improve your current practices in design, production, and marketing.

Telecommuting for Lawyers. Discover methods for implementing a successful telecommuting program that can lead to increased productivity, improved work product, higher revenues, lower overhead costs, and better communications. Addressing both law firms and telecommuters, this guide covers start-up, budgeting, setting policies, selecting participants, training, and technology.

Through the Client's Eyes, Second Edition. Includes an overview of client relations and sample letters, surveys, and self-assessment questions to gauge your client relations acumen.

Wills, Trusts, and Technology. Reveals why you should automate your estates practice; identifies what should be automated; explains how to select the right software; and helps you get up and running with the software you select.

Winning Alternatives to the Billable Hour: Strategies that Work, Second Edition. This book explains how it is possible to change from hourly based billing to a system that recognizes your legal expertise, as well as your efficiency, and delivery winning billing solutions—for you and your client.

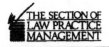

CUSTOMER COMMENT FORM

Title of Book:_____

We've tried to make this publication as useful, accurate, and readable as possible. Please take 5 minutes to tell us if we succeeded. Your comments and suggestions will help us improve our publications. Thank you!

1. How did you acquire this publication:

☐ by mail order   ☐ at a meeting/convention   ☐ as a gift

☐ by phone order   ☐ at a bookstore   ☐ don't know

☐ other: (describe) _____

Please rate this publication as follows:

	Excellent	Good	Fair	Poor	Not Applicable
Readability: Was the book easy to read and understand?	☐	☐	☐	☐	☐
Examples/Cases: Were they helpful, practical? Were there enough?	☐	☐	☐	☐	☐
Content: Did the book meet your expectations? Did it cover the subject adequately?	☐	☐	☐	☐	☐
Organization and clarity: Was the sequence of text logical? Was it easy to find what you wanted to know?	☐	☐	☐	☐	☐
Illustrations/forms/checklists: Were they clear and useful? Were there enough?	☐	☐	☐	☐	☐
Physical attractiveness: What did you think of the appearance of the publication (typesetting, printing, etc.)?	☐	☐	☐	☐	☐

Would you recommend this book to another attorney/administrator? ☐ Yes ☐ No

How could this publication be improved? What else would you like to see in it?

_____

_____

_____

Do you have other comments or suggestions? _____

_____

_____

Name _____

Firm/Company _____

Address _____

City/State/Zip _____

Phone _____

Firm Size: _____ Area of specialization: _____

We appreciate your time and help.

Fold

BUSINESS REPLY MAIL

FIRST CLASS   PERMIT NO. 16471   CHICAGO, ILLINOIS

. POSTAGE WILL BE PAID BY ADDRESSEE

AMERICAN BAR ASSOCIATION
PPM, 8th FLOOR
750 N. LAKE SHORE DRIVE
CHICAGO, ILLINOIS 60611-9851

Fold

ABA AMERICAN BAR ASSOCIATION

ABA Law Practice Management Section

Access to all these information resources and discounts – for just $3.33 a month!

Membership dues are just $40 a year – just $3.33 a month.
You probably spend more on your general business magazines and newspapers.
But they can't help you succeed in building and managing your practice
like a membership in the ABA Law Practice Management Section.
Make a small investment in success. Join today!

☑ **Yes!** I want to join the ABA Section of Law Practice Management Section and gain access to information helping me add more clients, retain and expand business with current clients, and run my law practice more efficiently and competitively!

Check the dues that apply to you:

❑ $40 for ABA members ❑ $5 for ABA Law Student Division members

Choose your method of payment:

❑ Check enclosed (make payable to American Bar Association)
❑ Bill me
❑ Charge to my: ❑ VISA® ❑ MASTERCARD® ❑ AMEX®

Card No.: _____ Exp. Date: _____

Signature: _____ Date: _____

ABA I.D.*: _____
(* *Please note: Membership in ABA is a prerequisite to enroll in ABA Sections.*)

Name: _____

Firm/Organization: _____

Address: _____

City/State/ZIP: _____

Telephone No.: _____ Fax No.: _____

Primary Email Address: _____

Get Ahead. 🏃

ABA Law Practice Management Section

**Save time
by Faxing
or Phoning!**

▶ Fax your application to: (312) 988-5820
▶ Join by phone if using a credit card: (800) 285-2221 (ABA1)
▶ Email us for more information at: lpm@abanet.org
▶ Check us out on the Internet: http://www.abanet.org/lpm

AMERICAN BAR ASSOCIATION

750 N. LAKE SHORE DRIVE
CHICAGO, IL 60611
PHONE: (312) 988-5619
FAX: (312) 988-5820
Email: lpm@abanet.org

I understand that Section dues include a $24 basic subscription to Law Practice Management; this subscription charge is not deductible from the dues and additional subscriptions are not available at this rate. Membership dues in the American Bar Association are not deductible as charitable contributions for income tax purposes. However, such dues may be deductible as a business expense.

Membership Application